Thinking Theologically

Thinking Theologically

Foundations for Learning

Eric D. Barreto

Fortress Press
Minneapolis

THINKING THEOLOGICALLY
Foundations for Learning

Cover image: Antishock/123RF
Cover design: Laurie Ingram

Library of Congress Cataloging-in-Publication Data
Print ISBN: 978-1-4514-8341-3
eBook ISBN: 978-1-4514-9421-1

The paper used in this publication meets the minimum requirements of American National Standard for Information Sciences — Permanence of Paper for Printed Library Materials, ANSI Z329.48-1984.

Manufactured in the U.S.A.

This book was produced using PressBooks.com, and PDF rendering was done by PrinceXML.

Contents

Contributors

Cláudio Carvalhaes is associate professor of preaching and worship at McCormick Theological Seminary. Originally from Brazil, he is an ordained pastor in the Presbyterian Church (USA). He is the author of *Eucharist and Globalization: Redrawing the Borders of Eucharistic Hospitality* (2013) and several articles on theology, liturgy, and preaching.

Stephanie Buckhanon Crowder is director of theological field education at Chicago Theological Seminary. She is an ordained Baptist and Disciples of Christ minister. She is author of the "Gospel of Luke" in *True to Our Native Land: An African American New Testament Commentary* (Fortress Press, 2007) and "Sociology of the Sabbath" in *Soundings in Cultural Criticism: Perspectives and Methods in Culture, Power, and Identity in the New Testament* (Fortress Press, 2013).

Jessicah Krey Duckworth is program director in the Religion Division at Lilly Endowment Inc. and an ordained pastor in the ELCA. She is the author of *Wide Welcome: How the Unsettling Presence of Newcomers Can Save the Church* (Fortress Press, 2013).

Mariam J. Kamell is assistant professor of New Testament at Regent College, Vancouver. She is coauthor of a commentary on *James* (2008) as well as author of numerous articles on the general epistles.

Amy Marga is associate professor of systematic theology at Luther Seminary in St. Paul, Minnesota. She is the author of *Karl Barth's Dialogue with Catholicism in Göttingen and Münster* (2010) and translated Karl Barth's *The Word of God and Theology* (2011).

Matilde Moros is assistant dean for special programs, director of field education, and instructor of Christian social ethics at New Brunswick Theological Seminary. She is a ruling elder in the Presbyterian Church (USA) and author of several articles on ethics and higher education.

Lance J. Peeler is the music director and organist at Southminster Presbyterian Church in Glen Ellyn, Illinois, and teaches Christian thought at Wheaton College. His research interests include United States hymnody, Anglican chant, and nineteenth-century Christianity.

Adam Ployd is assistant professor of church history and historical theology at Eden Theological Seminary. He is the author of several articles on the theology of Augustine of Hippo.

Jennifer M. Shepherd is an adjunct faculty member teaching biblical studies at Master's College and Seminary and a leadership consultant for ENGAGE Consulting, which focuses on denominational leaders and faith-based organizations in Toronto, Canada. Her first book, *Same Seed, Different Soil, and the Faith that Grows*, is due for publication in early 2015.

Introduction

Eric D. Barreto

My five-year-old daughter helped me think about thinking recently.

I was editing the essays found in this book when she insisted on collaborating on a new book together. How could I say no? So we gathered all the necessary supplies and got to work. She set about designing a cover. She needed a little bit of help writing out the book's title: *Thinking Book*. When the time came to illustrate the cover, she was a bit stumped. I encouraged her to draw a picture of someone thinking. Still flummoxed, she eventually concluded, "We're thinking about thinking. That's hard." She was right. This is hard work.

After all, the odd thing about thinking is that we barely have to think about thinking in order to think.

Let me explain.

Your brain is constantly at work. Whether you are asleep or awake, aware or zoning out, exercising or resting, your brain is a buzz of activity. It is guiding your movements, synthesizing new information, recalling old data.

Think about it this way. You are breathing at this very moment, aren't you? If you start thinking intentionally about your breathing, you will find yourself thinking about breathing as you compel your lungs to expand. You may even notice the complex physiological exertions breathing requires. But remember: even as you are reminding your body to breathe at this very moment, in a short while, you will forget to remember to breathe. And yet you will continue to inhale and exhale because your brain will pick up the slack. Imagine the intellectual burden we would carry if we had to *think* about breathing and digestion, healing and sleeping. Our brains are marvelous creations, never stopping their meticulous work until the day we draw our last breath.

And yet that's not exactly the kind of *thinking* we want to talk about in this book. The thinking that regulates breathing and practices habits and leans on instinct doesn't actually require much thought or intentionality on our part. That kind of thinking is usually not a powerful source of transformative theological and personal reflection and change. It won't necessarily shape and reshape the work of ministry to which you have been called. It probably won't be tested and honed as you work through seminary.

The kind of thinking we do discuss this in the book is intentional and potentially transformative. It is much more than my brain's sometimes feeble, sometimes inspiring machinations. The thinking we discuss in the chapters that follow is thinking about the God of the universe, the world God has created, and God's many children who populate it. Thinking theologically is hard work, for it seeks to discern the very source and sustenance of life: the God in whose "mind" we were first an inkling, the God who "thought" us into existence, the God whose "thinking" sustains us at every turn. Our thinking poignantly reflects God's own image. And so our thinking can help us participate in God's reign.

At the same time, we know that our thinking can be flawed, errant, unduly biased, prejudiced, sinful. Thinking theologically requires training and education certainly. But most of all, we lean on the Spirit when we think theologically. This is the Spirit God has promised will accompany us whenever we call on God. Paul writes in Romans 8:26: "Likewise the Spirit helps us in our weakness; for we do not know how to pray as we ought, but that very Spirit intercedes with sighs too deep for words." As Amy Marga explores in her essay "Thinking Systematically," thinking theologically is a prayer, a yearning for the Spirit to help us, as much as it is an act of the intellect.

Like *Reading Theologically,* this volume draws together the reflections of nine writers. They all share a common vocation: teaching people like you to think and grow and be in a rapidly changing world for the sake of the good news of Jesus Christ. Moreover, they are all excellent scholars who are seeking to hone our knowledge and understanding of a God whose grace and magnitude we cannot exhaust. In their diverse approaches, however, they share some important ideas, ideas we hope will dwell in your hearts as you study, and as you struggle and rejoice in your learning.

1. *Thinking theologically is as embodied as it is cerebral.* Thinking is not the exclusive domain of the brain. Certainly, the neurological work of learning and contemplation happens between our ears. But our brains are not severable from our bodies. Our brains are very much a part of our bodies. And so thinking is not just a cerebral act but also an embodied interaction with the world. Thinking theologically does not just deal with abstract thoughts and theoretical notions. Thinking theologically also requires us to see and touch and taste the world

that God has created. In short, we think not only with our brains but also with feet that guide us to strange places, hands that serve our neighbors, ears that listen to songs of joy and regret alike.

2. *Thinking theologically is as emotional as it is intellectual.* When we think theologically, we exercise the whole breadth of human experiences. Thinking theologically is not just a matter of learning facts, reading arguments, or writing informative essays. Thinking theologically also involves our spirits and our hearts. Thinking theologically calls us to love what we learn and grieve that sometimes our answers are wholly insufficient to the task of ministry. Sometimes all our thoughts will culminate in a faith that asks for God's help. Thinking theologically means that we see failure as a painful but indispensable part of following a path of faith, that we can measure ourselves not just by the grades we receive but also by the relationships we can foster with the help of a God that draws us together.

3. *Thinking theologically is as relational as it is individualistic.* To put it bluntly, you can't think theologically by yourself. We don't measure our theological acumen by participating in some sacred version of *Jeopardy.* Instead, thinking theologically drives us to our intellect in order to draw us to our neighbors. Thinking theologically does not require us to retreat into our studies and dwell in our minds; instead, it compels us with an insatiable curiosity to know and love one another—even and particularly those who differ from us.

In short, thinking doesn't just happen in that intricate collection of nerves and nodes in your skull. Thinking is not just a matter of dwelling alone with lofty thoughts. Thinking is not just a matter of accumulating bits of trivia or even collecting a wealth of theories. Thinking theologically also draws us to others, for how else will we know the world and know God? Thinking theologically draws us to our deepest fears and hopes, to the depths of despair and the heights of joy, to failure and risk. Thinking theologically, that is, thinking about God, is as human as anything else we do. And for this reason God draws near to us when we think in this way, for God's Spirit dwells whenever and wherever we gather together in faith and seek the face of God. Thinking theologically is about discerning a God who loves, cherishes, and exults in all our particularity; who shares our deepest griefs; who tastes our pain; who will not be limited by our imagination or hide from us.

Thinking can sometimes be akin to breathing. We are constantly engaged in processing data and sensory inputs all around us even when we are not conscious of the many neural pathways our minds are traveling. So, taking a step back to ponder the dimensions and practices of a particular way of thinking is a challenge. Even more important, however, is cultivating the habits of mind necessary in a life of ministry. Thinking theologically invokes an embodied set of practices and values that shape individuals and communities alike. Thinking theologically demands both intellect and emotion, logic and compassion, mind and body. In fact, this book will contend that these binaries are actually integrated wholes, not mutually exclusive options.

Thinking theologically is, I hope, something that will become as ingrained in you as breathing. Perhaps you will be so shaped by God's Spirit, so loved by God that your every thought will be infused with God's graciousness and justice, your every word marked with hope and expectation, your every deed surrounded by God's love. When we think theologically, we live theologically. When we think theologically, we exit the life of the mind and enter God's creation.

1

Thinking Mindfully

Jennifer M. Shepherd

In January 2011, mall surveillance cameras captured video of Cathy Cruz Marrero falling into the mall's main water fountain as she was walking and texting. It was a funny video, people laughed, and it brought to our attention the dangers of walking and texting. Ms. Marrero's accident could have happened to anyone, and even though her embarrassment led her to contemplate a lawsuit against the person responsible for posting the video online, she admitted she had learned a lesson when interviewed by NBC's George Stephanopoulos on *Good Morning America*.[1]

> **Stephanopoulos:** And, Cathy, I know that you—as embarrassed as you are from all this, you did learn a big lesson, huh?

> **Marrero:** Absolutely. Absolutely, George. Do not text and walk, especially to the younger generation. The fountain could have been

---

1. "Fountain Lady Fights Back," *Good Morning America*, http://lybio.net/cathy-cruz-marrero-good-morning-america-fountain-lady-fights-back-lawsuit/people/.html.

empty. I could have been in the hospital. I could have walked into a bus. You know, gotten hit by a car. It can happen anywhere. Anywhere.

And it is happening. Statistics show that walking and texting accidents are rising quickly in the United States. In fact, some towns like Fort Lee, New Jersey, are passing legislation that imposes fines of eighty-five dollars for residents caught walking and texting. There are numerous words to describe people as they walk and text: distracted, unaware, engrossed, oblivious. And if you are distracted, unaware, engrossed, or oblivious in an unfamiliar place and you are looking down, your next experience may be looking up from your phone in the middle of a mall water fountain.

But in Ms. Marrero's case, this was not just a matter of being unfamiliar with the landscape. She works in that mall. She was not in a new place. She was very familiar with her surroundings. She had navigated that same mall corridor for years. But this time, while walking and texting, she encountered the unexpected.

Stephanopoulos: Cathy, let me say, right at the start, I get it. When I saw this video, I said this could be me, but can you just take us back to that moment? What happened? What were you thinking? And what made you realize that you had a terrible fall?

Marrero: I realized I was falling when I was in the water already. Unfortunately, I didn't have anything to grab on to and hold my balance.

Stephanopoulos: From looking at the video, you look pretty composed for someone who just fell in a fountain in the middle of a mall. You got out, picked yourself up. What happened next?

Marrero: I was probably more dumbfounded. I was like, well, I'm hoping nobody saw me. So, let me just walk away. A kind lady of a store there, manager at the mall, was kind enough. I walked up to her. And all I kept saying was, "I fell. I fell. I fell in the fountain. I fell in the fountain. I fell in the fountain."

Marrero lost her situational awareness and fell in a place where she felt comfortable and confident. The jarring realization of what had happened—that she had fallen—was compounded by the truth of where it had happened, in a familiar setting. This is what left her shaken, disoriented, in disbelief, and, in her own words, dumbfounded.

Inherited Faith and the Moment You Look Up

At some point, every person will experience a moment when he will "look up" from his inherited faith tradition. It is unavoidable in this postmodern North American culture. It is disorienting in its unexpectedness. It is isolating in its uniqueness for each individual. You look up as if hearing something for the very first time: "What did you just say?? You look up with furrowed eyebrows in concern: "Do you really mean that?" You look up because you want to protest: "That doesn't make any sense."

Encountering the unexpected in a seminary classroom is an unavoidable hazard for students. It may not be as dramatic as falling into a fountain, but it will happen. It is unavoidable because in seminary, as in life and ministry, students become aware of their partial perspectives, are asked to reflect upon the influence of their religious traditions, and are challenged to consider the various interpretive options for belief that may and do exist. In these moments, the bodies of knowledge about God, which have been handed down to you, no longer seem secure. Something is always lost when you look up. Stability. Confidence. Naiveté. But much more is waiting to be gained when you can learn to think mindfully about your inherited faith traditions and the development of your personal beliefs.

When I refer to inherited faith traditions or bodies of knowledge about God, I am referring to the work of Ninian Smart and the six-part definition or scheme of study he established as the dimensions of religion: the experiential, the narrative, the ritual, the doctrinal, the ethical, and the institutional.[2] Knowing these six religious bodies of knowledge and what they establish as foundational for belief can be very insightful in the moments you look up; they can help you understand the range of theological beliefs you will encounter in seminary and active ministry. These categories can help because your religious community has appealed to one of the six bodies of knowledge, in varying degrees, and has influenced what you believe and the evidence you accept as reliable.[3]

2. Ninian Smart, *The Religious Experience of Mankind* (Englewood Cliffs, NJ: Prentice Hall, 1969), 15–25. Ninian Smart, the world-renowned expert in the study of religion as a nonconfessional, methodologically agnostic discipline, what most universities offer as Religious Studies, proposed that whatever else religions may or may not be, whether theistic or nontheistic, they possess certain recognizable elements, which can and should be studied. The study takes its place in the secular academy, where it draws heavily on anthropology, sociology, archeology, psychology, and other disciplines.

3. *Experiential bodies of knowledge* emphasize making a personal connection with God and accept feelings, emotions, and personal experiences as foundational for theological belief. You may look up if someone explains that they believe something about God because they have felt it or experienced it. *Narrative bodies of knowledge* emphasize how profoundly true, understandable, relatable stories, regardless of whether they are provable through the scientific method or defy common sense or logic, are foundational because testimonies reveal and explain theological belief. You may look up if someone explains that they believe something about God because that's just what the Bible says. *Ritual bodies of knowledge* emphasize the successful expression of belief found in repetition, standardization, and performance as foundational for belief so that participants benefit. You may look up if someone explains that they believe something about God because that's what God requires. *Doctrinal bodies of knowledge* emphasize certainty found in intellectual reasoning, systematic thinking, and prepackaged truths as foundational for belief. You may look up if someone explains that they believe something about God because it's the truth. *Ethical bodies of knowledge* emphasize relational behavior found in obligations, responsibilities, rules, and punishments as foundational for belief. You are expected to act in certain ways toward others. You may look up if someone explains that they believe something about God or are doing something because God watches and will judge our actions as good or bad. *Institutional bodies of knowledge* emphasize the role the religious group play in and the influences they exert upon society as foundational for belief. People may identify as defenders or adherents of the faith (church), as volunteer or individual participators in faith (denomination), as reformers of faith (sect), or as inventors of faith (cult). You may look up if someone is defending Christianity against change or advocating that we investigate new ways

In seminary, most students are only just becoming aware of their inherited traditions when they encounter the unexpected in the form of a different body of knowledge. It need not be the end of faith if you question or reject the bodies of knowledge of your inherited faith, since one body of knowledge is not the whole of the Christian message. However, the experience of looking up from your inherited faith can be just as dramatic as Marrero's, not just because of *what* is happening but also because of *where* it is happening. Such an experience is disorienting in its unexpectedness. You think that you are in a familiar, safe place—a seminary—doing a familiar, safe thing—studying the Bible—and *bam*! You fall and you look up as if hearing something for the first time. *Did your professor just provide experiential knowledge for discussions on healing in the New Testament when you expected logical, doctrinal answers?* You fall and you look up with furrowed eyebrows. *Do you look around the room wondering how other students find ethical standards in Leviticus that they want to apply today when you just find a story from an ancient culture?* You fall and you look up because you want to protest. *That doesn't make sense to me! Why are you trying to fix what isn't broken?* You don't see anything coming. You don't realize that you are falling until you fall. When you finally do get up, you may appear composed, but your confidence has been severely shaken, leaving you disoriented, confused, and dumbfounded. Such an experience is isolating in its uniqueness for each individual because our beliefs about God are deeply held and very personal. When Marrero fell into the water fountain, she was disoriented, embarrassed, and defensive. In the same way, the range of initial emotions that will arise in a seminary classroom—shock, sheepishness, fear, aggravation, irritation,

to do church. You may look up if someone is asking questions and calling for reform within Christianity or claiming that an entirely new vision is now required.

astonishment, embarrassment, concern, confusion, delight, even humor—can highlight the realization that most of us aren't prepared to explain or defend our beliefs beyond how we *feel* about them.

Thinking mindfully about theology and faith allows you to embrace this moment of being shaken, disoriented, and in disbelief as real and important and potentially educational. When you can acknowledge your emotions and reactions and allow those reactions to highlight the truth that the story you tell about God has been influenced by certain evidence, you are prepared to begin to think critically about theology and faith. You can come to understand why someone else thinks differently, engage those other views in healthy dialogue, evaluate your faith traditions, and add your voice to the discussion. You do not need to stay in a shaken, disoriented, disbelieving, and dumbfounded state nor do your feelings, which are powerful and real, necessarily have to lead to the death of belief. Rather, thinking mindfully can begin a process that can and should enable a person to look up, back, and again at her inherited faith so that its strengths, weaknesses, influences, and tendencies might be acknowledged. Richard Kearney has suggested that this process be labeled "anatheism," for the word denotes "repetition and return."[4] When you learn to look up, back, and again at your beliefs, you have a way to return to belief after the unavoidable, unexpected, and isolating experience of not knowing or, as I have explained it, falling.

---

4. See Richard Kearney, *Anatheism: Returning to God after God* (New York: Columbia University Press, 2010). This process begins with what is secure (theism), passes through the loss of that security or a death-of-God moment (atheism) or the not-knowing moment (agnosticism), but does not have to lead to the death of belief. I appreciate Kearney's emphasis that people today need a way to return to belief in God after having a dreadful and disorienting moment of "not knowing."

Learning to Think Mindfully When You Look Up

Whatever issue, topic, theory, or interpretation has caused you to look up, this is the starting point for mindful thinking. The experience of discomfort and strong emotions as you struggle to understand how someone else does not see things the same way you do will begin to highlight the influence of your inherited faith traditions and explain why you feel passionate about something that someone else considers to be a minor detail. The practice of being mindful is an important concept in most spiritual traditions, ranging from practices that meditatively empty the mind to practices that focus introspectively on the mind.[5] Mindfulness is a third way of knowing (awareness) that complements rational and sensory knowledge with subjective experience.[6]

Let me share two quotes that can help you understand the mindfulness I am advocating. The first anonymous inspirational quote is this: "Don't shush your inner voice. It's who you really are." When you are mindful, you are aware of feelings that are occurring in the moment, and you take them seriously for the information they provide without trying to alter or manipulate the experience. Pleasant reactions are enjoyable, making you feel agreeable. You will naturally desire to discuss issues that make you feel agreeable. Unpleasant reactions are displeasing and offensive, making you feel disagreeable. You will naturally desire to shut down discussions of issues that make you feel disagreeable. Neutral reactions are disinteresting and

---

5. The term *mindfulness* and many current mindfulness practices generally associate with the meditative traditions of Eastern religions. Thinking mindfully is not primarily concentration meditation (the practice of focusing, quieting, or emptying the mind of judgment), and it is not primarily introspection (the process of reflectively looking inward at one's own thoughts and emotions). It is a combination of intentional focus and awareness of emotions.

6. Bob Stahl and Elisha Goldstein, *A Mindfulness-Based Stress Reduction Workbook* (Oakland: New Harbinger, 2010). The two forms of meditation are insight and concentration. Mindfulness meditation is considered insight meditation.

disengaging, making you feel dispassionate. You will naturally tune out or ignore discussion of the issues you consider unimportant.

Practicing mindfulness in a seminary classroom is essential, because too often students regurgitate answers for marks or in support of denominational positions just to keep the peace. Holding your inner voice lightly, even if for a moment, does not change your inner voice or its influence but allows you to acknowledge that you have questions, doctrinal hang-ups, theological preferences, or alternative interpretive approaches.

The second quote, from Thich Nhat Hanh, is this: "Mindfulness is the capacity to shine the light of awareness onto what's going on here and now."[7] Remember, thinking mindfully *complements* rational and sensory thinking skills. When you are aware, you understand and have access to knowledge that you can use and apply to a situation. When you admit that you are experiencing a strong emotion, mindfulness allows you to take the next step and to investigate why you are feeling that emotion.

Why do you feel compelled to correct the teacher? Why do you feel the need to admonish another student to move on from a topic that you think is such a minor issue? Emotions are signals to pay attention to what needs attending to and are meant to alert us to what is going on. We must learn to respond accordingly to these emotions and do something about them. An important distinction should be noted here between *acknowledgement* of emotions and *acceptance* of emotions. To acknowledge is simply to see things as they are, whether you like it or not. Acceptance, on the other hand, is being at peace with things as they are.[8] I am not advocating that seminary students learn to accept all expressions of theology or suggesting

7. From Thich Nhat Hanh, *Peace Is Every Breath: A Practice for Our Busy Lives* (New York: HarperOne, 2011).

8. Stahl and Goldstein, *A Mindfulness-Based Stress Reduction Workbook,* 71.

that students suspend judgment on certain faith positions or refuse to evaluate their inherited faith traditions. Thinking mindfully is primarily a critical thinking skill that equips a student to acknowledge the strong feelings and emotions that are part of belief systems in a way that can simultaneously validate the student's personal faith journey choices and challenge her to consider the validity of the paths she has left untraveled on her faith journey. Thinking mindfully can work to develop confidence in your faith positions when you know you haven't allowed your emotions to dismiss or invalidate other options.

Learning to Think Mindfully When You Look Back and Look Again

I discovered the importance of learning to think mindfully about inherited faith traditions from my own experience and from the many conversations I have had with students over my twelve years of teaching. It was very early in my seminary training when I looked up from my inherited faith traditions. I had fallen, but I didn't know it until I was in the water. I didn't know where I was or how I got there. I was embarrassed, confused, apologetic, and angry. I finally looked back and again three years later and learned that I didn't have to apologize for or look back with suspicion on the religious traditions that had shaped my beliefs. But looking up plunged me into three years of struggle that destroyed two key ideas that had previously been firm and stable elements of my personal belief.

It happened in the second semester of my graduate studies in a class studying the book of Exodus. "What a fantastic book," my professor exclaimed, "with excellent examples of the early pattern of biblical storytelling: take a common and influential story that is already current in your culture (in this case the Mesopotamian hero myth and the law codes of the Mesopotamians and Hittites) and tell your unique story using the same format." On the first day of class, this all sat well with me because the part I heard most clearly was that the Israelites were telling their unique story using the common formats of the day. But by the third class, I began reacting, although I would not fully understand the root of my reactions for another three years. The class made me very aware of the book of Exodus as a story. I had always loved the fact that the Bible was full of stories and that we were reading the testimonies of people's experiences with God. But when all the possibilities for reading and comparing the book of Exodus were presented, I reacted to all the new ways people were telling the story and how they were finding meanings that I didn't think were there. I actually did throw up my hands in the air and exclaim, "Well, anyone can read anything they want from this text. How can anyone know for sure what the Bible is actually saying?"

Looking back and again at my inherited religious tradition three years later revealed that I was expecting a single, correct interpretation of the Bible. I assumed that with careful, diligent study you could and should eliminate all other interpretive options as illegitimate. In addition, I had been taught to be suspicious of human involvement in the writing, copying, and editing of the Bible and carried with me the idea that it must be endued with some supernatural element for us to trust it as God's revelation. When it became clear to me that my particular tradition was as thoroughly human as other traditions and that one particular method had been chosen (from among many) to read and interpret the Bible, I experienced a feeling of being set adrift, no longer being anchored, and I had very little confidence in any tradition's ability to answer religious questions with certainty.

When you experience moments like these, remember, *don't shush your inner voice.* I did shush my inner voice, which led me to stop giving my take on interpretive issues, since it was just an opinion and mine was no better than anyone else's. I was teaching during these years, and many times I told my students that when I would say, "I don't know," it was not that I didn't care about their questions. I really didn't know what the answer should be! I began to focus on possibilities and learned to provide information, lots of information, without venturing a conclusion. It was such a frustrating time because my intellectual world was growing and expanding, but I had no confidence to express my evaluations and was constantly reacting to what I was learning. I became certain of the uncertainty, and without any sense of confidence, I was miserable.

Remember my reference to anatheism? What had been secure (theism) was stripped away, and for three years I had passed through the loss of that security or a death-of-God moment (atheism). But in 2001, I was about to embrace a more tentative and chastened belief so that if I wanted to return to God, I could return to God. When I sat down with my doctoral advisor for the first time, he asked me if I felt prepared for this new phase of study. Knowing that my research skills were strong, I told him yes. And then I said, "I should tell you that my background is quite charismatic, but I can be very critical in my thinking." Without hesitation, he responded, "That's good, but you don't have to apologize for your background. It has made you who you are. You are going to see things in this text that others miss or have difficulty seeing. Your insights will be important to the discussion. But you may also miss what other people see. Just make sure you know why you tend to see things the way you do. That is always the challenge." In that moment, I felt that I finally had a place to stand again. In that moment, I learned three things that I incorporate into all my teaching and every conversation I have with people.

Don't apologize for your background. It has made you who you are. This is a liberating truth, even if you have chosen to distance yourself from certain parts of your inherited faith.[9] There is no need to be embarrassed, for all of us bring the influence of our background to our reading of the Bible, our theologies, our ethics, and our spirituality. My inherited faith had emphasized narrative knowledge and influenced me to accept Bible stories as true without questioning the logic or scientific possibility of the events. As a result, I fought against the suggestion that parts of the story from Exodus were not unique or supernatural. Maybe it will take you longer than your classmates to look up, but you are you and your moment will not be the same as their moment. Do not be embarrassed that you did or still do believe what you believe.

You will see things others miss or have difficulty seeing. But you may also miss what other people see. Embrace that you have looked up because someone has failed to see what you see, and admit that you, in turn, might not see what he or she sees. My inherited faith did not see great value in encouraging new understandings of spiritual truth but sought to defend status quo interpretations. As a result, I missed seeing other interpretive possibilities in the Exodus text. What is clear and obvious to you is not a given to everyone else. What is pleasant to you may be offensive to someone else. What so obviously caused you to look up may never be obvious to someone else. There is no eagle-eye view available to anyone.[10]

9. There is no need to apologize that you have looked up, for everyone shares the same reality: "understanding the nature of subjectivity, that our responses are created out of who we are, allows us to see that others read and respond according to the same logic; we deduce from what we bring with us: the baggage, light or heavy, of our lives." Laurence Musgrove, "What Happens When We Read: Picturing a Reader's Responsibilities," *JAEPL* 11 (Winter 2005–2006): 52–63, esp. 56.

10. "Everyone stands (mostly subconsciously) within a particular tradition and historical context that influences their personal horizons. Understanding is a product of our language, our history, and our traditions. These 'prejudices'—these prejudgments—offer us our lens on the world. We do not have available the eagle eye, the Enlightenment's dream of detached reason that

Make sure you know why you tend to see things the way you do. Why did I tend to see things the way I did?[11] My reactions began to make sense. I tended to think about things in terms of "correct" and "incorrect" categories. Plus, my confidence was linked directly to my ability to identify which arguments and reading belonged in which category. Whenever I learned about or evaluated other interpretations, I was focused on eliminating those interpretations in favor of one correct interpretation. I reacted to other reading approaches because I was beginning to wonder about the necessity of, even the existence of, a single "correct" meaning. Once I realized that all the different readings and interpretations I encountered in my studies were not random or merely wrong but flowed out of another person's tendency to see things in a certain way, I began to understand how to evaluate another interpretation with more generosity and curiosity.

Mindfulness is the capacity to shine the light of awareness onto what is going on here and now. Acquiring this knowledge of myself (what I was seeking, what I was reacting to, why I was struggling) was the only way I could renew and review the beliefs I held so dearly and return to God. I was not going to outrun my interpretive tendencies. I like to have the facts and be confident when I speak. It was not going away. I tend to eliminate options to arrive at a solid conclusion. I would always be restless until I was able to understand why I needed to be confident about my interpretation.

Looking up from inherited faith can be a devastating experience for students and teachers alike, but a mindful approach acknowledges

is independent in perspective. Understanding is always located within the situated and partial perspectives of our prejudices. Our understanding is shaped by the way we belong to the world." Francis, J. Mootz III and George H. Taylor, eds., *Gadamer and Ricoeur: Critical Horizons for Contemporary Hermeneutics* (New York: Continuum, 2011), 1.

11. "How each of us reads the Bible is partly the result of family, neighbors and friends (a socialization process), and partly the God-given accident of long-term development in faith." Walter Breuggemann, "Biblical Authority," *The Christian Century*, January 3–10, 2001, 14–20.

that all reactions, even unpleasant ones, are signs of life reflecting the foundations of personal faith and belief. Looking back and again can energize you with a new appreciation for the religious tradition in which you were reared, a recognition of the positive and negative influences that your tradition brought to your personal faith, and the skills and ability to embrace and understand the influence the tradition has exerted in your life.

Thinking Mindfully Develops Confident and Conversational Seminarians

A seminary student who learns to think mindfully about beliefs learns to acknowledge his own reactions and emotions as important influences on his beliefs. A seminarian who learns to think mindfully can admit that she has an internal monologue and a bias that allows her to be more patient as she listens to someone, to be less apologetic as she puts forth her own beliefs, and to be genuine in her expression of empathy. Consider that the experience of looking up highlights the level of passion and the insights you will bring to discussions of belief and faith. But acknowledging presuppositions does not mean that you cannot believe in something with confidence or that all faith is illusory. Looking up, back, and again alerts you to comfort zones and natural preferences. Knowing your limitations actually works to create confidence in your views and openness to the positions of others.[12]

---

12. "Sometimes it is thought that, once the existence of presuppositions has been recognized, presuppositions should be abandoned altogether, as far as possible, and that our approach to the text should that of an 'open' (or empty) mind. Not only is such a goal unlikely to be achieved, but also it is doubtful whether an attempt to shed presuppositions or preconceptions is always the best way of achieving openness to the text." David J. A. Clines, "Biblical Hermeneutics in Theory and Practice," *Christian Brethren Review* 31, 32 (1982): 65–76, esp. 70.

Only you will know the circumstances that lead to that profound, exhilarating, dreadful, liberating, or startling moment when you look up from the religious beliefs of your inherited faith system. Embrace the moment you look up, knowing that emotions are vital elements of belief. You can relate to the one-third of the population that is struggling to work through some theological or emotional issue of Christian faith.[13] You can help these people think mindfully about their faith by reminding them that God is not repulsed by our negative feelings. But it is also true that God wants us to process those emotions and choose how to respond so that we can be in relationship with God and neighbor alike.

Evaluate the moment you looked up knowing that your expectations lead you to walk away from certain beliefs and to walk toward other beliefs. In this way, you can relate to the 80 percent of the population who desires to be known as "spiritual" as opposed to "religious" and reject denominational certainty in favor of a spiritual journey. You can help them think mindfully about the paths and traditions they are embracing, rejecting, or merging. You can relate to the majority of Americans who "have a gnawing sense that there is more to the spiritual life than they are experiencing" and are open to discussing, debating, and questioning theology and faith.[14] You can help them think mindfully about their quest to discover for themselves just what truth is and how to apply it to their lives.

What options are then available for us when we reach this moment of discovery? I am challenging you to consider more than the usual options: theism, atheism, or agnosticism. Your moment of discovery is a chance to learn about yourself: who you are, what evidence persuades you, and why you react. In the process, our attempts

13. George Barna, *Futurecast: What Today's Trends Mean for Tomorrow's World* (Austin, TX: Tyndale, 2011), 125.
14. Ibid.

to understand the deep values of others may affect our own understanding of truth and right in subtle and significant ways.[15] We can begin to recognize our individual preferences knowing that the better we understand our point of view and expectations, the better we will be able to articulate our position and still allow for dialogue on other points of view.

15. Richard Moon, ed., *Law and Religious Pluralism in Canada* (Vancouver, BC: UBC Press, 2008), 6, www.ubcpress.ca/books/pdf/.../LawandReligiousPluralisminCanada.pdf. Our understanding of the values and concerns of others (religious or otherwise) will always be approximate or partial, but we may have the capacity to give practical meaning to them and to reach some form of agreement or understanding.

2

Thinking Bodily

Lance J. Peeler

Too often when we think about thinking, we think only about our brains. But that is only part of the story.

Brains are not some abstract reality, floating in nothing. They are not purely analytical machines (a common trope in science fiction, from C. S. Lewis's *That Hideous Strength* to the Star Trek episode "Spock's Brain," to the French film *The City of Lost Children,* and many others). Rather, brains are housed within bodies. These bodies affect how brains function and think, and more than just in the way bodies sustain them. Sure, bodies need food, water, rest, exercise, sunshine, and any number of other things to sustain our lives. They are also engaged in our intellectual pursuits. Thinking is more than just our brains—our whole bodies are involved in thinking, the same way that they are involved in eating, running, or resting.

The good news is that God created us to be embodied beings. God did not make disembodied souls to float around in eternity with the Godhead. Instead, God created us with bodies. Even after these bodies die, we also, as the creeds remind us, look for the resurrection of the dead. As I sometimes have to remind my students, this is a bodily resurrection, not a resurrection into nothingness. God not only created us with bodies but also experientially understands how these bodies function, because Christ experienced it in the incarnation. Christ was born, grew up, and experienced a whole human life. Christ himself experienced a bodily resurrection, described in 1 Corinthians 15:20 as "the firstfruits of those who have fallen asleep." His resurrected body bore the marks of the crucifixion, as Thomas found out—so it was still a physical body, even if changed.

These physical bodies affect how we think and function. We cannot leave them behind and think without them. We always think bodily. Thinking bodily takes many different forms and looks different for people of different traditions. In the Christian tradition, perhaps the most important way that we think bodily is in worship. After we consider what it means to think bodily, we will turn to how worship is the most distinctive and embodied way that Christians think bodily. After all, worship that engages our own bodies and the bodies of others is the ideal way to form us into people that love God and love others.

Thinking Bodily

James K. A. Smith makes the case in his books *Desiring the Kingdom* and *Imagining the Kingdom* that it is what we love that truly determines what we think about and how we function in the world.[1] For the most part, we do not spend our time analyzing available data and making decisions based on this data. Instead, we do things out of

---

1. James K. A. Smith, *Desiring the Kingdom: Worship, Worldview, and Cultural Formation* (Grand Rapids: Baker Academic, 2009) and idem., *Imagining the Kingdom: How Worship Works* (Grand Rapids: Baker Academic, 2013).

habit, and we build our habits in seeking and doing things we love. When I biked to the local coffee shop to write, I did not look at my bike and think about balancing, pedaling, and where to go. I put my computer in its bag, strapped it on, and started going. I didn't have to think about where to go; I already knew the way. My body is used to riding my bicycle and knows what to do without having to stop and think about it.

One more example: I am an organist, and I don't think about the mechanics of playing the organ each time I do so. In fact, it's when I think too hard about those mechanics that I start to make mistakes. My body knows what to do, and if my brain gets in the way, my fingers and my feet can't do what they are supposed to do. My fingers are so accustomed to playing music that when I am thinking about a particular piece or thinking about how a new song I've heard goes, I find my fingers twitching to play the right notes. Or if I am struggling to figure out how a piece I've heard goes, allowing my fingers to play, even without a keyboard in front of me, helps me hear it in my mind, because the physical action of playing is so ingrained in my experience of music.

I could list any number of examples, because we all function this way. We do most things by habit, from sitting down in a chair to cracking eggs to make breakfast or giving a good friend a hug.

But, you might be thinking, giving someone a hug is quite different from playing J. S. Bach's *Well-Tempered Clavier*—and you would be partially correct. It is in practice that things become habits, and some things take more practice than others. Years of practice are what let pro basketball player Kevin Durant make his shots without thinking or radio host Terry Gross interview someone without lots of "ums" and awkward silences. When you see your friend, the first thing you do is give a hug, because that's what you do. These habits that come from practice affect how you interact with the world, how you process information. They affect your very being, at a more basic level than thinking through ideas or facts.

These habits are highly affected by other people's bodies and experiences as well. I grew up in Oklahoma, a conservative, religious, sparsely populated state. I spent my twenties in graduate school in New Jersey, a liberal, diverse, densely populated state. The habits and ways of thinking to which I was accustomed because I grew up in Oklahoma were challenged and sometimes changed by my time in New Jersey. The constant interaction with people from all over the world broadened my experiences, as almost everyone I knew growing up was from Oklahoma or at least the surrounding states. Living in close proximity to thousands of people changed my habits of driving, biking, walking, and making room for people while doing these things. Each of these states shapes the people I know from both places in that so many of my friends from Oklahoma have huge houses and acres to live on while so many of my friends from New Jersey have small apartments or houses with tiny yards. And yet, both see their living situations as normative.

Thinking Bodily through Prayer

It is not just living situations that affect how we think, though. How we pray and worship has an enormous impact on our lives. The Orthodox theologian Alexander Schmemann reminds us in *For the Life of the World* that people are created to be worshiping beings.[2] All cultures around the world have a form of prayer. If you do not regularly spend time in prayer, you are missing some of what it means to be human and much of what it means to have a relationship with God. Prayer is a habit that, as you attend seminary, must be

2. Alexander Schmemann, *For the Life of the World: Sacraments and Orthodoxy* (Crestwood, NY: St. Vladimir's Seminary Press, 2002), 118.

practiced. Seminary will challenge your beliefs and ways of thinking. We all grow up thinking in certain ways due to the places where we grow up, our families, our friends, the churches we attend. A good education helps to broaden those ways of thinking, both in ideas presented and habits formed. These habits might include writing a persuasive paper, crafting a good sermon, baptizing an infant or an adult, but, without the habit of prayer, these other practices of thought and being can become overwhelming.

Prayer can take many forms. I grew up as part of the Baptist tradition, in which spontaneous prayer is the only way to pray. Written prayers were meaningless to those in the church my family attended. Only prayers "from the heart" were effective. There is great power in praying without any written text in front of you. It allows you to spontaneously tell God what is on your mind, what struggles and concerns you have, and what joys you are experiencing in your life. You can allow the Holy Spirit to lead you as you pray and wind up in all sorts of interesting places. If you practice spontaneous prayer, it's also easy to pray at any time and any place. You don't need to have a book with you or have prayers memorized. Spontaneous prayer helps you deepen a relationship with God and also with others if you practice it in group settings.

Spontaneous prayer is an important way to speak to God. But using written prayers is also important. While my wife and I were teaching in rural Indiana, we joined the Episcopal Church—a church that largely uses written prayers. Written prayers are powerful in sometimes surprisingly different ways than spontaneous prayers. If you pray the daily office, the prayers that you pray daily become part of your thinking. The prayer of confession from the *Book of Common Prayer* reads as follows:

Most merciful God, we confess that we have sinned against you in thought, word, and deed, by what we have done, and by what we have left undone. We have not loved you with our whole heart; we have not loved our neighbors as ourselves. We are truly sorry and we humbly repent. For the sake of your Son Jesus Christ have mercy us and forgive us; that we may delight in your will, and walk in your ways, to the glory of your Name. Amen. [3]

This prayer has become part of how I confess. It makes me consider if I have truly loved God with my whole heart and if I have truly loved my neighbor as myself (the answers to both of which, too often, are no). The experience of praying that prayer, day after day, week after week, has shaped how I experience the world. Is what I am doing really helping me to love God with my whole heart? Is this action showing love to my neighbor? And, as the lawyer asked Jesus in Luke 10:29, "Who is my neighbor?"

If you practice praying with written prayers, you never are stuck without anything to pray. There are always reminders for you, reminders that take the form of your own self, people you know, your city, and on up through the entire world. Written prayers help to remind you that the church you are a part of is, as the Creed says, truly catholic. People around the world and throughout time have prayed the same or similar prayers.

Too often, we think about prayer—whether written or spontaneous—as simply a head exercise. While it's true what my Sunday school teacher taught me—you really can pray anywhere, while you're doing anything—it's also a good idea to have more practices than just thinking toward God.

A Russian Orthodox friend once told me a story about a man who went to his priest, saying he was considering atheism. The priest told him to go home and pray every morning for thirty days, laying prostrate before his icons. The man reluctantly agreed. At the end of the thirty days, he came back, and his faith was restored. As captured

3. *The Book of Common Prayer* (New York: Oxford University Press, 1979), 360.

by this story, my friend and his tradition understand something about people. Praying involves more than just our heads but rather involves our whole bodies. Orthodox prayer involves written prayers, candles, incense, and icons as a reminder of the great cloud of witnesses that prays with us. Often, physical action is called for, from laying or kneeling, as in the story, to venerating icons or raising hands. Praying with our whole bodies can help prayer become a habit. Kneeling, praying with palms up to heaven, raising hands, laying prostrate—all are things to do with our bodies that can help us get into the habit of prayer.

Thinking Bodily through Worship

Prayer is not simply an individual practice, however. It is wonderful to pray by yourself, in your room with the door shut, as Jesus commends in Matthew 6:5-6. But praying with other Christians is absolutely vital. Worshiping with other Christians is important as Scripture reminds us repeatedly, Hebrews 10:24-25 most explicitly: "Let us consider how to provoke one another to love and good deeds, not neglecting to meet together, as is the habit of some, but encouraging one another, and all the more as you see the Day approaching."

The best worship services involve our whole bodies. Alas, many churches today are unfortunately focused solely on the head. There might be a few songs at the beginning that the congregation might or might not sing along with, followed by a forty-five-minute sermon that fully engages the mind but leaves out the rest of us. Much can be learned from such a service, but we are not disembodied heads, and worship that treats us as such doesn't allow for full participation by the worshipers.

Worship has traditionally been so much more—a much longer affair, certainly—but in cutting things down to fit nicely into an hour, too often everything but the intellectual part has been cut out. Worship that engages our whole selves involves excellent music, movement by the worshipers, the waters of baptism, the taste and smell of bread and wine at Eucharist, the smell and feel of oil, the fragrance of incense, and any number of other things. For instance, in Jesus' time, temple worship was a fully multisensory experience, with the people having to journey into the temple where they experienced the smell of burning sacrifices, the sound of trumpets and choirs, the sights of the grandeur of the temple itself. As the Christian church's worship developed, ornate, beautiful buildings became common; processions were used at important points; incense indicated holiness; and the Eucharist became the central point of the service. Instruction was important, certainly, but it was not the primary task. Worshiping God was the central purpose. Only after the Reformation did some churches take Sunday worship and turn it into a lecture, out of nervousness over the purported excesses of the late Middle Ages and Renaissance.

Fortunately, some churches are recovering the arts in worship. Music has been common in most traditions to varying degrees, even after the Reformation. Imagery, drama, dance, and the other arts are being recovered in many places from which they have been absent. Beauty as expressed through the arts draws people in and allows them to reflect on God's beauty. Truth and goodness are important parts of worship; without beauty, they cannot feed people's whole selves. The Swiss theologian Hans Urs von Balthasar understood beauty's important relationship with truth and goodness. Writing in the 1960s, he says:

> We no longer dare to believe in beauty and we make of it a mere appearance in order the more easily to dispose of it. Our situation

today shows that beauty demands for itself at least as much courage and decision as do truth and goodness, and she will not allow herself to be separated and banned from her two sisters without taking them along with herself in an act of mysterious vengeance. We can be sure that whoever sneers at her name as if she were the ornament of a bourgeois past—whether he admits it or not—can no longer pray and soon will no longer be able to love.[4]

As you attend seminary, I hope you can find a church that appreciates beauty and its importance in feeding your whole self; and once you finish seminary and are serving your own church, you can help that community feed people's whole selves.

Churches are also recovering the importance of the sacraments, which for Protestants usually means baptism and Eucharist. Baptism is traditionally seen as the first step of being in fellowship with the church. For some churches, it has remained extremely important; for others, people might attend a congregation for years and yet never be baptized. Baptism is a wonderful rite, for the external rite of cleansing with water signifies an internal cleansing. The sign is obvious to what it signifies, especially for those churches that practice immersion or submersion. It also fully involves the person being baptized—there are questions to answer, prayers to pray, the waters of baptism themselves, and, often, the oil of chrism, asking for the Holy Spirit's power. Baptism is a whole-body experience!

Similarly, the Eucharist (or Communion or the Lord's Supper, depending on your tradition) is a full-body experience. We do more than just think about Jesus when we take Communion. In many traditions, the worshipers leave their seats and come to the altar or table, reminding people of the importance of coming to Christ. In others, people pass bread and wine to one another, reminding them of the fact that all believers are called to be priests. Then, we eat and

4. Hans Urs von Balthasar, *The Glory of the Lord: A Theological Aesthetics*, ed. Joseph Fessio and John Kenneth Riches, vol. 1, *Seeing the Form* (San Francisco: Ignatius, 1982), 18–19.

drink things of which Christ said, "This is my body" and "This is my blood." You don't have to believe in transubstantiation to know that these elements are more special than simple bread and wine. Jesus calls us to feast with one another and with him. This is the chief way that on a regular basis we affirm the normal functions of the body in worship. Maybe we should be doing more than having "oyster crackers and grape juice," as I once heard a wedding coordinator so unceremoniously put it.

Worshiping with body and soul affects all of life. Regular worship—weekly and daily, communal and individual—forms us into people for whom all of life becomes worship. It forms us into people who love God. You might think that you already love God, as is likely, if you're going to seminary. Worship helps to nurture and deepen that love. In seminary, you spend so much time studying theology, Scriptures, church history, pastoral care, and any number of other subjects. The barrage of information can be overwhelming. Regular worship, especially worship that engages your whole self, helps to maintain that center of love for God. It also helps to draw you together with others, many of whom might be quite different from you.

One of the best things about seminary is the interaction with fellow students and faculty from different backgrounds, different denominations, even different nations. You will disagree with some of them—it's impossible not to do so. Their own places of origin, cultures, genders, races, and worship practices will affect how they think, even as your own have affected you. Worshiping with people who are different from us reminds us that we are called as many members of one body and that the body needs those different members.

As you begin seminary, find a place to worship that will engage your whole self—not just your mind. Worship together with your classmates in chapel, too. Many seminaries have field education placements in which you'll be serving a church and learning from the staff there. Think about the community your church is in and how their backgrounds might differ from your own. Don't think that you alone have great knowledge to impart to that community. You have much to share with them, but what God calls you to share cannot be captured solely by the intellect. Instead, think about what you can learn from the people as you practice being in community with them. God may also be calling you to learn from others and their stories.

The good and bad of thinking bodily is that we always do it, even if we don't realize it. As you begin seminary, much of your time will be spent doing the same things over and over: reading, writing, studying, or listening to lectures and sermons. Doing these things as intensively as seminary requires will form you into a person who can do them well. As you practice them, participate also in those practices that will form you into a person who will love God and love people, for they are made in God's own image. Only by making those things a habit can you love God and people fully, which is our primary calling as people of faith.

3

Thinking Pastorally

Jessicah Krey Duckworth

When our high school would let out early, my friends and I would walk nearly a mile straight down Seventeenth Street into Center City Philadelphia to hang out for the afternoon. On occasion, we'd catch a regional rail line one stop away to the mall and spend our babysitting money on hair clips and chocolate. More often, though, we'd hang out at the food court in the transportation hub, mingling with the downtown professionals and shop clerks on their lunch break. After a few hours of carefree leisure, my friends and I would hop on our designated trains, subways, and buses to go home. I attended a magnet school that pulled students from every neighborhood in the city. My best friend lived forty minutes away from me. The first time I ever visited her house was in college. Having grown up in major urban areas, city life shaped my relationships and my perceptions about the world I lived in. Everything I cared about was in the city. When I left high school for college, I dreamed of becoming an urban planner. I wanted to be a part of creating the world I loved.

Church was another part of my urban world. I have been shaped deeply by the practices and ministries of long-standing, multiracial, urban congregations. The faithful people in these congregations taught me to pray fervently for peace and to expect justice in the world God loves. Little did I know back then that the sisters and brothers in my church community had taught me my first lessons in practical theology.

At its core, practical theology is an activity of believers; anyone who reflects upon God's action in the world connected to the circumstances of their daily life is a practical theologian.[1] Christian believers live life and respond to situations going on around them as they do, because they have encountered God presently acting in their lives and in the world.[2] For instance, during our congregation's prayers in worship, I heard a woman give thanks to God for the safe return of her young adult granddaughter who had stayed out late without calling home first. This grandmother prayed, "God, I know you would have given me a sign if something had been wrong, so I knew in my spirit that she was okay. But I thank you for bringing her home safe." Sunday after Sunday, I heard petitions like these that included joys and concerns about families and friends, anxieties about the safety and education of the children in Philadelphia, and hopes for peace and reconciliation across the war-torn regions of the world. Through the speaking of these prayer petitions, followed by conversations in Bible study and fellowship hour, and intermingled with bulletin announcements and personal invitations to provide food for those in need, to volunteer for social services agencies, or to participate in rallies or letter-writing campaigns to local politicians, I heard earnest convictions shared that God's kingdom was breaking

1. Bonnie J. Miller-McLemore, *Christian Theology in Practice: Discovering a Discipline* (Grand Rapids: Eerdmans, 2012), 106–7.
2. Andrew Root, *Christopraxis: A Practical Theology of the Cross* (Minneapolis: Fortress Press, 2014), 91–92.

in and that justice for all people was imminent. But more than simply hearing these confessions in church, I saw faithfulness in action too. What was shared on Sunday morning was a reflection of people living out of their convictions that God's work in the world happens through the hands of God's people, serving one another and the world.

"To be a Christian at all is to be a theologian. There are no exceptions."[3] This is a claim that Howard Stone and James Duke make in *How to Think Theologically*. "Every aspect of the life of the church and its members is a theological testimony. So too are the particular ways Christians have of relating to what is around them, their styles of interacting with others and the world."[4] To be called a theologian might feel strange for Christian believers living out their vocations in the world God loves. You might think that theologians, both in the past and in the present, are specially trained to give lectures and write books about the Christian faith, relating the essential truths of the biblical witness and the history of the church to Christian life today. Though accurate in some historical contexts, the locus of theological reflection has shifted considerably over the centuries. Bonnie Miller-McLemore notes that the historical separation between the household and the university that has informed latter-day theological reflection ought not to be absolute.[5] The place of Christian theology in the believer's household and in their daily life has a long tradition in Christianity.

3. Howard W. Stone and James O. Duke, *How to Think Theologically* (Minneapolis: Fortress Press, 1996), 2.
4. Ibid.
5. Miller-McLemore, *Christian Theology in Practice*, 105.

Locating Practical Theology

Practical theology occurs at the bedside of a child reflecting with her parent on what the word *evil* means during a nightly routine of sharing the Lord's Prayer. Practical theology occurs when a young-adult group on a mission trip gathers after their day of repairing houses to wonder aloud about the injustice of privilege and poverty and the brokenness of God's world. Richard Osmer calls these single-setting, short-term activities *episodes*. An episode is "an incident or event that emerges from the flow of everyday life and evokes explicit attention and reflection."[6]

Another focal point for practical theology occurs when believers are called to respond to more complex *situations*, such as at the bedside of a dying woman who, encouraged by her hospice volunteer, reconciles with her brother after twenty years of not speaking. Unlike episodes, which are short term, "a situation is the broader and longer pattern of events, relationships, and circumstances in which an episode occurs."[7] Situations are best understood through narrative.

The third focal point of practical theological interpretation, according to Osmer, is a *context*. When practical theology analyzes a context, it is calling attention to the ways social and natural systems interact with one another to give rise to a given situation.[8] It is this contextual analysis that often occupies the time of groups and committees in all kinds of religious organizations working together to figure out how to take the next faithful step together.

6. Richard R. Osmer, *Practical Theology: An Introduction* (Grand Rapids: Eerdmans, 2008), 12.
7. Ibid.
8. Ibid.

Living Practical Theology

Every Sunday morning for four years in college, I walked from my dorm room at George Washington University past the White House to a Lutheran church four blocks farther north on Vermont Avenue for worship. Within this congregation, I was surrounded by people who welcomed me like family even though I was far away from my own. Early in my time in this church, I learned about its rich historical commitment to those citizens of D.C. with the most pressing needs.

When riots broke out in Washington, D.C. in 1968 after the assassination of Martin Luther King, Jr., Luther Place Memorial Church kept its doors open, providing shelter and food for nearly ten thousand people, even as other congregations in the area barred their doors with armed guards out of fear. Luther Place is most well known for its faith-based social service agency, which has been providing short- and long-term shelter for women experiencing homelessness since the 1970s. This agency, known as N Street Village, is a continuum-of-care facility that also provides case management, substance abuse treatment, employment services, and affordable housing.

When I later started an internship at N Street, I also served on a visioning team to develop a theological study center there. The dream of Luther Place was to encourage seminary professors, students, and congregational teams to visit N Street to learn about the issues surrounding homelessness, social advocacy, and urban ministry. We wanted visitors to explore the complex social and natural systems leading to poverty and homelessness in the city through the voices and stories of N Street residents and to place their narratives into conversation with God's justice. In other words, we were doing practical theology.

Practical theology happens when a community of believers discerns how to align their activity in the world with God's activity in the world. An important step in this process is to observe, collectively, the ways in which God acts in the world. Communities are necessary because no individual alone can address the complex situations that arise today. I define community specifically as people who acknowledge that their shared work is to gather regularly to develop meaningful resources.[9] When done as a community, practical theology seeks to collect the diverse individual convictions each participant has about God's work in the world into a shared resource that can then guide the community's action. A faith-based community, doing practical theology, insists that God's nature and God's action in the world are essential components of the community's task of discerning and acting. Resources developed by faithful communities draw the community's observations into relationship with the biblical and theological reflections of past communities as well.

Many communities try to figure out how the community should continue its present activity and move into the future without considering God's work and engaging biblical and theological resources. The visioning team for the study center was made up of individuals with professional skills in drafting a business plan, creating marketing and communication strategies, attending to personnel matters, and developing an advisory council and bylaws. This knowledge and skill was vital for developing the study center, and it might have been tempting to create an action plan with these professional contributions alone. However, each member of the visioning team was also motivated to participate in this community because of their convictions about God's justice in the world.

9. Duckworth, Jessicah Krey Duckworth, *Wide Welcome: How the Unsettling Presence of Newcomers Can Save the Church* (Minneapolis: Fortress Press, 2013), 66–72.

Meeting together regularly, we worked to surface our implicit understandings of God's justice. At the encouragement of a couple of longtime members of the church and the current pastor, we also read through an essay by a previous pastor who framed the ministry of Luther Place and N Street Village through a biblical theology of hospitality. With helpful resources from the past, we created a more explicit and compelling biblical and theological vision for the study center and its programs that was grounded in God's radical hospitality and justice and that could guide our future work together.

In retrospect, I remember that this process felt extremely slow.

Developing a deliberate strategy for moving forward as a community of faith is time intensive. For many communities, the temptation is to describe a situation and move as quickly as possible to a potential action. To rush too quickly from describing a problem to figuring out the solution is common in faith-based organizations, which often lack time and resources for more careful reflection. Unfortunately, however, hastily made decisions generally replicate the status quo and lack theological imagination or potentially risky yet Spirit-led possibilities. Slowing down allows communities of practical theologians to complexify episodes, situations, and contexts through critical reflection on multiple levels. John Swinton and Harriet Mowat explored the significance of complexifying situations:

> Most of us tend to live within situations in ways which are unreflective and uncomplicated. Many of the aspects of our situations are experienced as nothing more than background noise. It is only when problems arise through crisis or our engaging in a process of complexification that the complicated nature of our situation emerges. . . . A key aspect of the practical theological task is to evoke such "unnatural self-reflection" and to raise people's consciousness to previously hidden dimensions of everyday situations.[10]

10. John Swinton and Harriet Mowat, *Practical Theology and Qualitative Research* (London: SCM Press, 2006), 13

What is necessary is to slow down the decision-making process and complexify it—which for some, especially a twenty-year-old college intern, can feel like an eternity!

There is always the danger that the complexity of a situation will render the group incapable of making a decision and moving forward. Finding an appropriate balance between complexity and action is the necessary task of leaders and communities trying to figure out God's desires for the shape of their work.

Reimagining Practical Theology

Over the last few decades, a consensus has been developing around a particular process for complexifying practical theological interpretation and moving faith-based communities toward strategic action. This consensus model for interpreting situations consists of four mutually interrelated and yet clearly distinguishable tasks. In *Practical Theology: An Introduction*, Richard Osmer defines these four tasks, calling them descriptive-empirical, interpretive, normative, and pragmatic. Osmer offers that these tasks can be performed either informally or through a more structured, formal process.

The first task of practical theological interpretation is the *descriptive-empirical,* or asking, what is going on? and gathering as much information as possible to describe the episode, situation, or context. Generally, the first task of practical theology emerges because a context has changed, leading to episodes and situations arising that need the community's attention. A faith community can often feel overwhelmed as it is called to attend to many different situations. This is where leadership is necessary to help the community decide how and when it is going to respond to some emerging reality. When something happens or emerges that calls for a response, it is important for the community to gather and share with one another what they perceive to be happening around them. Informal description can take the form of listening to members of the community explain their thoughts, perceptions, and feelings about a particular situation. Depending on the scope of the situation, however, a more formal description might be warranted at times. Designing a more comprehensive research agenda to describe *what is going on* with interviews, focus groups, and data collection, for instance, can provide a thorough investigation into a complex problem. Collecting information through more formal means can help the community refine a problem and identify possible theories that can be explored to understand the problem better.

The second task of practical theology sets the description within a wide variety of perspectives and disciplines, asking, why is this happening? This is the *interpretive* task. Informally, interpretation can take the form of thoughtfulness, which means, as it implies, to be considerate toward others in difficult situations and to stay curious about the situation and offer insight into the more complex aspects of the situation from a variety of perspectives. More formally, the task of interpretation can draw upon theories within other disciplines such as psychology, economics, neurobiology, or anthropology. For instance, one could explore the vexing problem of a congregation's dwindling church attendance from a human resources framework because the church has been without a pastor for two years or from an economic perspective that describes the changing work patterns among adults in the community leading to more adults working on Sunday mornings. Without acknowledging both variables, the diagnosis of the church's issues could be wholly wrong. The more theoretical frames available, the more the community can be curious and invite complexity into a situation.

The third task seeks to discern God's guidance by attending to the Spirit as well as the Christian norms and texts that might guide the situation. This *normative* task asks, "What should be going on in light of God's being and work in the world?" *This is the most crucial task in practical theological interpretation.* Recall that in the process of developing the study center, each person participating in the visioning conversations had implicit notions of how justice and hospitality could frame the work of N Street and the study center. But the harder task was to render explicit those implicit notions so that the whole community could participate in the construction of the normative vision and move forward. Osmer suggests that the informal way to approach the normative task is through sympathy for the world God loves.[11] In this normative task, the community confesses together that God is not abstract and distant from human situations, but rather in Jesus Christ God comes near to the pain, suffering, and brokenness in the world, caring mightily, yet intimately, for who we are and what we do. This sympathy takes a more formal turn as contemporary communities reflect on the ways historical religious communities have heard God's promises in the past and lived into God's vision for humanity and creation. Engaging the biblical witness, the church's history, and even discovering excellent Christian practices in other communities close at hand and around the world can lead communities toward developing strategies for what they ought to do in light of God's desire to reconcile the world. Responding to God's movement toward the world in Jesus Christ, practical theology helps Christian communities discern how to live faithfully in the world God loves.

The final task is *pragmatic* or *strategic* and seeks to guide and construct proposals for particular Christian activity in the future based upon all that was learned in the previous three tasks. This is ultimately where communities want to land. Yet churches so often

---

11. Osmer, *Practical Theology*, 136.

get caught in the paralysis of analysis and cannot move to action. Thus, this task calls specifically upon the leadership of a community to implement the proposed strategy. Leadership is key for moving along the whole process of practical theological interpretation. Yet like in the other tasks, two different kinds of leadership emerge at different times. More generally what is needed is *task competent* leadership for committees or small groups that helps a group of people stay on task and invites everyone's participation. Some situations, however, call for *transformative* leadership in which the whole of the organization undergoes deep transformation because it recognizes that it must respond to larger and more systemic change in context. Although transformative leadership is needed in many religious organizations today, religious leaders would be remiss if they underestimated the importance of performing task-competent leadership well.

The four tasks within this consensus model of practical theology can be depicted in a circle. (See figure 4.1.) Ultimately, because time and history move forward, communities will find themselves identifying a new problem or situation that will call for practical theological interpretation and the process will begin anew.

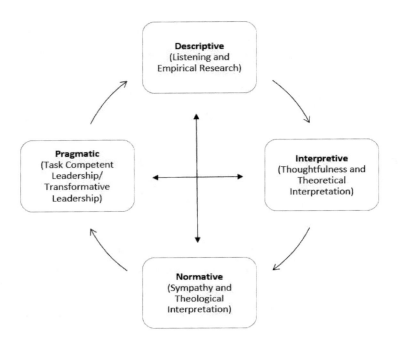

Figure 4.1. Practical theological interpretation[12]

As with many models being learned for the first time, this one will feel wooden for a while. For the novice practical theologian or first-time gathering of believers, it is helpful to slow down and interpret episodes, situations, and contexts by distinguishing each practical theological task in succession. That said, for the more experienced practical theologian or a community with a long history together, these tasks will over time appear smoother and more interrelated than distinguishable. Ultimately, the goal of theological education is to provide religious leaders with the resources they need to lead communities through these four tasks toward faithful action, followed by ongoing learning and reflection on that action that returns to the descriptive task to start again.

12. Ibid., 11.

Learning Practical Theology in Seminary

During my final year of college and with the encouragement of congregation members at Luther Place, I realized that I could combine my passions for God's justice with my love of the city if I became a pastor in an urban church. I started an MDiv program at the Lutheran Theological Seminary at Philadelphia with an urban concentration, intending to become a pastor serving an inner city congregation. Alongside my introductory courses in Hebrew Bible and systematic theology, I spent my Sundays traveling with the urban concentration cohort to six vibrant inner-city congregations. After worship, our cohort met with the pastors of these churches to ask them questions about their ministry. In our weekly reflection group with a mentor pastor, we considered together how the ministry in these congregations related to what we were learning in our courses. We were doing practical theology by *reflecting theologically on the practice of ministry itself.*

In addition to practical theology being an activity of believers and an activity of a community of believers seeking to discern faithful action together, it is also a curricular area in theological education.[13] In practical theology courses, seminarians learn to practice the arts of ministry. These courses include preaching, Christian education, youth ministry, pastoral care, leadership, worship, evangelism, and mission. Urban ministry, family ministry, chaplaincy, or other context-specific field education experiences may also be included in practical theology. These distinct arts of ministry can all be construed as subdisciplines of practical theology. While in seminary, you have the opportunity to explore the different subdisciplines in their specificity. Preaching and evangelism, for example, each have their own history, dialogue partners, methods, and practices. Leadership

13. Miller-McLemore, *Christian Theology in Practice*, 107.

courses might introduce you to historical and contemporary patterns of leadership in religious communities while encouraging you to consider the biblical and theological convictions that give shape to your own perspectives on leadership. Seminary courses in pastoral care will provide you with the theological and psychological frameworks to guide the caregiving response of a faith community.

Because these subdisciplines are taught as distinct courses, ministers and those working in faith-based contexts often perceive their daily tasks (caring, teaching, preaching, and leading) as discrete, isolated responsibilities that make up their professional work. The discipline of practical theology draws the arts of ministry into a larger framework. Practical theology as an overarching discipline works to identify what is common among the subdisciplines within ministry in order to provide a coherent and integrated approach to ministry. First and foremost, what is common is the consensus model of practical theological interpretation described by Osmer and presented above. But practical theological courses have other common commitments as well.

Curriculum revisions in theological education over the last ten years have sought to address this fragmentation among ministry responsibilities by teaching toward integration. Faculty who teach practical theology courses are leading this conversation in seminaries. In some seminaries, first-year courses now introduce students to the study of ministry and theology (much like this book in your hands) and capstone courses are offered in the senior year to provide formative moments for students to "claim their voices, authority, and knowledge of an issue" in a way that integrates identity, intellect and practice, as Kathleen Cahalan contends.[14] This integration taught in

---

14. Kathleen A. Cahalan and James R. Nieman, "Mapping the Field of Practical Theology," in *For Abundant Life: Practical Theology, Theological Education, and Christian Ministry*, ed. Dorothy C. Bass and Craig Dykstra (Grand Rapids: Eerdmans, 2008), 115.

seminary courses is still only a prelude to the work that is done after you graduate. In fact, one of the aims of these integration courses is to inspire lifelong learning, because the honing of your professional tasks takes years of practice and reflection on practice.[15]

Practical theology courses, no matter the subdiscipline, prepare you to lead communities in three ways. First, these courses help you name the presuppositions and life experience you bring to the tasks of pastoral ministry or leadership in a faith-based organization. Part of your work in seminary is to identify your natural inclinations and embedded confessions of faith for ministry so that you can be aware of the ways your preferences privilege certain frameworks and certain people. The more you are aware of your inclinations (such as my penchant for cities), the more flexible you can be as you adopt different practices on behalf of others.

Second, practical theology courses invite you to learn from practical experience in ministry, to learn from doing. These courses spend a great deal of time in practice with case studies, small-group role play, simulated projects and activities, and actual preaching and teaching, all of which encourage you to practice certain skills in a setting where learning happens explicitly. The knowledge that emerges from reflective practice is called practical knowledge. This is a knowledge our bodies learn to remember. Through courses in practical theology, you learn how to trust this embodied knowledge.

Third, practical theology courses prepare you to lead others involved in the tasks of ministry. As Pastor Peter Marty writes, "Pastoral leadership is not just a matter of fulfilling specific pastoral functions. It is a matter of performing these functions, and indeed every aspect of daily life and work, in a way that helps a strange menagerie of believers make sense of life as a communal enterprise.

15. Craig Dykstra, "Pastoral and Ecclesial Imagination," in Bass and Dykstra, *For Abundant Life*, 47.

It is about fostering a community that is in love with the possibilities of its togetherness in Christ and its responsibility of being available to the needs of others."[16] To be a practical theologian is to be in love with God's people, nurturing their faithful way of life embodied throughout the week in their day-to-day work and in their service to one another and to the world.

As you learn to see Christian life with the eyes of a practical theologian, you will see the Spirit's work everywhere. Practical theology is a discipline. Practical theology is a set of courses you will take in seminary. Practical theology provides you with a model to interpret episodes, situations, and contexts theologically. Practical theology happens when you participate in a community of believers seeking to discern faithful action together. Practical theology is at its core an activity of believers discerning how God's movement toward the world in Jesus Christ affects the way Christians move within the world—and for me, the city!—God loves. Where do you see practical theology in your life?

---

16. Peter W. Marty, "Shaping Communities: Pastoral Leadership and Congregational Formation, in Bass and Dykstra, *For Abundant Life,* 325.

4

Thinking Biblically

Mariam J. Kamell

Caricatures of Christianity are all too prevalent within and without the church. Sometimes, these caricatures are deserved. For instance, charges of hypocrisy can hit a bit too close to home when our practices fall short of our beliefs. Other times, these caricatures bear little resemblance to the actual practices of actual Christians.

And yet even among those claiming to be followers of Jesus, there is a wide diversity of familiarity with the ancient narrative to which we claim to belong. Unfortunately, biblical illiteracy is rampant in our churches. Some of us may know quite a number of select Bible verses, but a sense of context, of the whole story, is often missing. Yet, as we engage in critical thinking as Christians, one of the most important things we can do is allow the drama of Scripture to shape our thoughts and lives. But to become such people, people who act out of thoughtful knowledge born of our relationship with God and God's word, we have to know how our own story fits into the stories that have come before us, particularly those in the Bible. Our story and the biblical stories form a continual narrative of which we are just a part.[1]

It is a common move to point to Jesus' encounter in Luke 24 with two disciples on the Emmaus road as a pivotal postresurrection moment of revelation. However, we should not miss that Jesus begins by questioning the disciples' own reading of the biblical narrative. They knew their own stories to a certain extent, but they then interpreted them in light of the popular narratives around them: the Messiah must be one who would rescue Israel from the Romans, correct? And in that scheme, what place was there for the suffering and—even more mystifying—the death of Jesus?

But what does Jesus do? He could have revealed himself immediately, thereby saving those poor disciples an extra fourteen miles of walking in one day (out of and promptly back to Jerusalem). He could have reprimanded them for failing to believe the women. He could have responded in any number of ways, but what he did was teach his disciples to think biblically: "Beginning with Moses and all the prophets, he interpreted to them the things about himself in all the scriptures" (Luke 24:27 NRSV). Instead of revealing himself and telling them to figure out the narrative later, Jesus first taught them to see him in the word before revealing himself in the flesh.

Following the model of Jesus, we will begin by exploring the narrative into which we have been invited, looking at both what that narrative is and also what it reveals about the ways we understand who we were, are, and will be. Second, we will look at one of the skills necessary for thinking biblically: reading in context. *Context* is simply the fancy word that reminds us that if we are to think

---

1. N. T. Wright, *Paul and the Faithfulness of God, Book I* (Minneapolis: Fortress Press, 2013), 116, observes, "*The Bible was not merely a source of types, shadows, allusions, echoes, symbols, examples, role-models and other no doubt important things.* It was all of those, but it was much, much more. It presented itself as a single, sprawling, complex but essentially coherent narrative, a narrative still in search of an ending" (emphasis original).

biblically, we must pay attention to the whole conversation that we are joining, rather than cherry-picking and proof-texting to the detriment of truthful meaning. And third, if we take seriously the process of thinking biblically, then this will have an impact on how we live. If it does not, then we have not yet truly begun to think biblically.

Know Your Narrative—and Know Your God

So first, to be slightly provocative, we might observe—and ask why—Scripture was given to us as a long narrative, filled with stories about people whose names we cannot pronounce and historical details that may or may not be all that precise. Why is more of the Bible not like the Decalogue, a nice, neat list that summarizes what we need to know? Better yet, why did Scripture not come in the form of a systematic theology, first telling us all we need to know about God, then preemptively going ahead and filling in the bits about Jesus, the Spirit, the people of God, and other neat categories?

I suggest we take this question seriously, not because I think systematic theology is a bad discipline (it isn't) or that God decided the Israelites couldn't quite handle propositional truths (they very well could have) and so told them stories instead, but rather that if we are to take our Bibles seriously, then we have to take the form of the text seriously, perhaps as seriously as we take its contents. And by this, I'm not meaning literary form as in poetry versus prose versus apocalyptic but rather the larger genre of the Bible as an unfolding narrative of creation, fall, call, covenant, exile, redemption, and anticipated restoration. If we take the Bible seriously, we are in the narrative, and so we should understand what narrative we are in!

Our culture has a number of competing narratives. One is a narrative of endless economic growth and endless potential for success. Another is the story that there is no single story, just a variety of competing stories, and we all just have to accept each other's stories.[2] These competing narratives are not just found in the culture. The church itself has many stories. Whether it be prosperity as the gift of God or the necessity of speaking in tongues for salvation, we hear such defining stories constantly. Whether we are fully aware of their influence or not, these are stories that shape us to the very core, that teach us who we are, that create a map of our futures.

In the midst of all these stories, the God of the Bible reveals God's story of the world for us to read. In reading this story, we find our place within it. And we are warned—and have modeled for us—that at points this story will place us at odds with the stories surrounding us. This story gives us the courage and confidence to live faithfully. And more, the chronicle of a God who loved the world so much that God acted within its history repeatedly, finally coming into it and living and dying for it, should compel us into a deep love for God's creation and the people within it.

The biblical narrative teaches us the courage to live into a story that at times is sideways to our culture because the narrative of Scripture is deeply relational. The constant reiteration of the narrative is that God is faithful to God's own. As God reveals God's character in a deeply personal moment with Moses in Exodus 34, we discover who God is: "The LORD, the LORD, a God merciful and gracious, slow to anger, and abounding in steadfast love and faithfulness" (34:6). On the basis of God's revealed character, Moses can thus promise the Israelites, "Because the LORD your God is a merciful God, he will neither abandon you nor destroy you; he will not forget the covenant" (Deut. 4:31), and the Hebrew Bible ends with the promise,

---

2. For an excellent reading of some of the "myths" circulating in the modern stories that (mis)shape our culture's view of Christianity, I recommend Iain Provan, *Convenient Myths: The Axial Age, Dark Green Religion, and the World That Never Was* (Waco, TX: Baylor University Press, 2013).

"For as you return to the LORD, your kindred and your children will find compassion with their captors, and return to this land. For the LORD your God is gracious and merciful, and will not turn away his face from you, if you return to him" (2 Chron. 30:9).[3] The writers of the Hebrew Bible, across the generations, celebrate across the entire text the faithful character of YHWH, even while revealing and lamenting both the faithfulness and unfaithfulness of God's people.

And so God's people recognize the holiness of their God. Ezekiel has to endure the terrible sight of the glory of God departing the temple. Jeremiah warned of exile. Isaiah and Micah were infuriated by hypocrisy. Sin was so problematic because the God of Israel called God's people to "be holy, for I the LORD your God am holy" (Lev. 19:2, but also repeatedly throughout the book; see also Exod. 19:6 where God calls Israel to be a "holy nation"). As the representatives of YHWH on earth, they were to reflect God's character, and the failure to do so led to exile. At the same time, the judgment that accompanied exile was balanced with the covenant promise of restoration when they repented (cf. Deut. 30) and with the faithfulness of a God who keeps promises. And as we, as modern readers, come to know the God of the whole Bible, we see that God's holiness endures along with God's justice and mercy and compassion. YHWH consistently calls Israel to know God as the basis of their relationship, and often at those points God reiterates how God has acted toward them—because to see God act is to know God.

As we come to know the God of Israel through the biblical story, we read the Gospel accounts of Jesus with much more clarity. Instead

---

3. The Jewish Scriptures, known as the Tanakh, are arranged in a different order than the Christian Old Testament canon. They begin with the five books of Moses, followed by the prophets (the "former" prophets include Joshua, Judges, Samuel, and Kings while the "latter" include Isaiah, Jeremiah, and Ezekiel along with the twelve "minor" prophets whose work is actually considered one "book"). The final section is the "Writings," which includes the Psalms, wisdom texts, and the histories of the exile. The Tanakh thus concludes with Chronicles, reminding Israel of their story as well as God's promised faithfulness to God's chosen people.

of simply reading his miracles of calming the sea or the accounts of the sky breaking open at the baptism as nifty moments when Jesus shows off his miraculous power, we see YHWH acting in a way only God can to control the chaos of the sea and sky. We hear echoes of the exodus and exile being accomplished. And perhaps best of all for many of us, we recognize the constant thread of the fulfillment of YHWH's promise to Abraham, that through his descendants would come the blessing of all the nations, all of which are called to be in relationship with this holy God of Israel. The more we are immersed in the story, the more we will become people shaped to and by the story and by this God. It is through immersion in the story and coming to know the God who calls us into relationship that we become biblical thinkers. There is no other way.

Seek Context

I devoted so much attention above to the Hebrew Bible because, unfortunately, too many Christians in too many traditions tend to ignore these texts in favor of the New Testament. That is, however, to be functionally a Marcionite Christian, ignoring the entire first two-thirds of God's action in redeeming creation as well as tearing Jesus and Paul and the other New Testament characters loose from their contexts.[4]

As mentioned above, we read the Gospels differently the more we understand the Hebrew Bible. The more we read the entire Bible and expand our familiarity with the Apocrypha and pseudepigraphal writings as well as other Jewish texts, the better we can hear the

---

4. Marcion was a second-century theologian who argued that the God of the New Testament was different (that is, good and graceful and trustworthy) from the God of the Hebrew Bible. Marcion therefore rejected those writings and adopted a truncated New Testament canon. See A. G. Padgett, "Marcion," in *Dictionary of the Later New Testament and Its Developments,* ed. Ralph P. Martin and Peter H. Davids (Downers Grove, IL: InterVarsity, 1997), 705–8.

conversations going on in the Gospels, the epistles, and the prophets. And if we can be closely attuned to these conversations, we might just hear how God is speaking through the Scriptures rather than just having our assumptions reflected back to us. One helpful example of this kind of reading might be David Instone-Brewer's work on divorce and remarriage.[5] For him, expanded familiarity with rabbinic debates revolutionized his scholarship when he came to understand Jesus as engaging an ongoing debate among those who sought to teach Israelites. As such, Jesus' teaching on divorce (for example, Matt. 19) fits within a spectrum of ongoing discussions during his own time and do not necessarily reflect the entirety of his teaching on the subject.

It is worth remembering as we try to be biblically literate and thoughtful people engaging our modern culture that Jesus, Paul, James, John, or any other of Jesus' followers were not addressing directly the twenty-first century with its conversations and its problems. Some problems are ubiquitous: greed, pride, ignoring the poor. And yet our culture is a long, long way from the Judea of the first century in which Jesus walked and talked or the Greek and Roman world in which Paul ministered.

To think biblically means paying attention to the text, its historical and literary context as well as our current context. For one, we need to know the text, the story, as I argue above. But also, we need to realize that a secondary implication of the text as story means that the context in which events and teaching happen are also important. We cannot simply pull a verse out and proof-text it as support for our position nor can we simply pull a verse out and dismiss it as irrelevant. Thinking biblically means paying attention to how each part interacts with the whole, asking ourselves why it is there and

5. David Instone-Brewer, *Divorce and Remarriage in the Bible* (Grand Rapids: Eerdmans, 2002).

what purpose it serves. Before we dismiss parts we dislike or elevate parts we like, we must listen well enough to the text to find out how it might have been heard by its first audiences, as best as we can discern. To think biblically requires us to be willing to submit ourselves to the text, even when we don't like what it seems to be saying. It requires us to listen long enough to hear the voice of God in God's word. Biblical interpreters come to many conclusions about these texts, and so we cannot claim to have come to the inerrant interpretation of a particular text. In fact, the varied conclusions of people who have listened long, even while they may disagree, tend to breathe an air of the grace of God in their arguments.

And third, just as Jesus engaged in debates that were ongoing and the "hot topics" of his day, we cannot afford to be Christians who castle ourselves into our towers and pray for the rapture to take us away. Those who are shaped by the narrative come to see themselves as part of the narrative. As such, they might be a Deborah, called to act as judge in a patriarchal society or the unassuming Jael who rescues Israel from an oppressive king. Or they may be called to be Moses, uncertain of his qualifications but elevated nonetheless, or Ezekiel, who sat for seven days in deep distress upon receiving his calling, but obedient nonetheless to rebuke his wandering people. What we come to realize as we steep in the story is that God works through faithful people to shape, change, and call God's world. While we wait (often in vain) for politicians to make changes in governance to protect the widow, the orphan, the foreigner, and the poor, God often works by calling unexpected people to be the hands and feet of God's grace. Indeed, it is precisely the widow, the orphan, the foreigner, and the poor who can break open our experience of God's compassion. While we may be uncomfortable with conversations about sexuality, divorce, or abortion, we come to realize that it is through God's people that God calls God's church not only to holiness but also—and always—to love and mercy.

The biblically shaped people of God will continue the conversations of Jesus, engaging the hot topics of our day, even though there may not be explicit teaching in the Bible about them. There undoubtedly will be disagreement on what is the "correct" resolution to pernicious problems and the "most loving" response to intractable situations. To be a biblical thinker means we must engage our culture. In a globalized world, we need to be careful listeners who seek to understand our varied contexts, narratives, and identities and how identity markers such as race and gender shape our narratives and perspectives. We must know our context in order to interpret an ancient text that continues to breathe life into our communities. To do otherwise is to fail to appreciate that it has always been through God's people that God has worked to bring God's kingdom. Even when God worked in dramatic, miraculous ways, God brought Moses to work with and for God. Similarly, Jesus called twelve ordinary, awkward, impulsive, scared men into the center of his reshaping of history, and then left them, and us, to the continued work of turning the world right side up.[6]

Let Your Heart Burn (or Hearers versus Doers)

That said, to be a biblical thinker is to be a biblical doer. One cannot be one without the other. As Jesus says to the legal expert in Luke 10:28, "You have answered correctly. . . . Do this and you will live." All the correct theology we can know and teach, all the Bible verses

---

6. To see this in action in the book of Acts, I'd recommend Kavin Rowe, *World Upside Down: Reading Acts in the Graeco-Roman Age* (Oxford: Oxford University Press, 2010). I also recommend Andrew Walls, *The Missionary Movement in Christian History* (Maryknoll, NY: Orbis, 1996), especially chapters 1 and 2 regarding the shifts that Christianity has made to its varied contexts.

we can memorize and recite, serve us in no way unless we do them. "Do this and you will live." Maybe I focus on this as part of being a biblical thinker as a result of specializing in the epistle of James, but to me it seems evident that we cannot claim to be thinking in a biblically correct way when we stop short of letting the text shape us, shape our loves, and shape our actions.

Dietrich Bonhoeffer, in a most profound critique of such shallow thinking in Christendom, observes:

> I can therefore cling to my bourgeois secular existence, and remain as I was before, but with the added assurance that the grace of God will cover me. It is under the influence of this kind of "grace" that the world has been made "Christian," but at the cost of secularizing the Christian religion as never before. . . . The Christian life comes to mean nothing more than living in the world and as the world, in being no different from the world, in fact, in being prohibited from being different from the world for the sake of grace. The upshot of it all is that my only duty as a Christian is to leave the world for an hour or so on a Sunday morning and go to church to be assured that my sins are all forgiven. I need no longer try to follow Christ, for cheap grace, the bitterest foe of discipleship, which true discipleship must loathe and detest, has freed me from that.[7]

How resonant are the words of 1 Peter 4, which observe that the neighbors of Peter's audience are "surprised" that the Christians no longer join them nor act like them, and as a result they slander the believers. Peter seems to think it likely that his audience will suffer for following Christ and encourages them accordingly. In this, he follows his Lord, who gives a warning in the beatitude "Blessed are those who are persecuted for righteousness' sake, for theirs is the kingdom of heaven" (Matt. 5:10). For some reason, we skip this beatitude and the one that follows: "Blessed are you when people revile you and persecute you and utter all kinds of evil against you

7. Dietrich Bonhoeffer, *The Cost of Discipleship* (1959; repr., Norwich: SCM Press, 2001), 10.

falsely on my account. Rejoice and be glad, for your reward is great in heaven, for in the same way they persecuted the prophets who were before you." (5:11-12). And yet what the biblical narrative shows us is that often the ones whom the text affirms for their love of God are also the ones in a minority position, unpopular, and even slandered.

Those who think in line with the biblical text know that it is not merely the hearing of the words and knowing them that makes any difference. Truly biblical thinkers are doers of the word, not hearers only (James 1–2). This flows through the whole of the text, from the call (and later reprimand) on Israel to live in accordance with their knowledge of the character of God and God's laws for God's people to Jesus' desire that his disciples live according to God's love in the world (cf. John), to James's challenging prose that argues the point Bonhoeffer picked up two millennia later. Toward the end of his excellent book on the epistle of James, Richard Bauckham warns against the hypocrisy of those who would study the epistle and endlessly write about it and yet never actually follow its teaching.[8] The danger of biblical and theological studies is the endless nature of the wordsmithing and word games we can play that lead us from ever actually having to put the word into practice. We study the text endlessly to the avoidance of ever following that study to its logical conclusion: obedience.

However, it is also worth considering the character of biblical thinkers, or to put it another way, to consider the how of living in the world against the grain. When we choose to live according to the kingdom of God in the here and now, live right side up in an upside-down world, we can do so in an abrasive way that bolsters our pride and our self-righteousness. "See?" we may say. "I am not

---

8. Richard Bauckham, *James: The Wisdom of James, Disciple of Jesus the Sage* (London: Routledge, 1999), 184.

simply studying, I am proclaiming the truth in opposition to all my culture. I must be faithful!" Simply to be in the minority does not indicate the righteousness or rightness of one's interpretation. To take pride thus fails to take into account the model of our Savior who somehow drew to himself sinners, prostitutes, tax collectors, and others whom society deemed unworthy of God's love. None of them appear to have remained the same after their encounter with Jesus; however, his transformative call was not done through hostile abrasiveness but a profound demonstration of the character of God in its mercy and holiness. This also means that when there are profound disagreements on the shape of Christian mercy, we must never lose sight of the image of God in those with whom we disagree and love them with every fiber of our bodies even while we disagree. In such a way, perhaps disagreements can become charitable and productive and demonstrate to the world hospitality in the body of Christ.

To be faithful biblical thinkers, we must be shaped by the very character of our God. We cannot be dominated by the pride or judgmentalism so common in our world and too many of our churches, but we also cannot be wallflowers who refuse to make the jump from text to life. We must speak the word of God boldly, proclaiming the good news of the gospel into a world in need of the hope provided by a coherent alternative narrative to those provided by our world. And we must accompany that speaking with the actions befitting a people of the God who provides justice for the widow and orphan, aid for the poor, and a home for the landless. To be biblical thinkers is to be biblical actors, shaped to the character of our God and attuned to the needs God brings before us. To be anything other than a doer of the word reveals that we have not yet heard it correctly.

5

Thinking Historically

Adam Ployd

By the time I went to college, I had seen enough Discovery Channel specials to know what Christian history looked like: a distortion of the pristine teachings of Jesus through two thousand years of oppressive patriarchal conspiracies best narrated by a deep voice speaking over ominous, foreboding music. So I majored in religion, intending to deconstruct the naïve Christianity with which I was raised. In my biblical classes, I exulted in discovering inconsistencies in the Gospels and promoting the "original" meaning of biblical texts over the "misinterpretations" of later tradition. The past was a problem, and I was going to solve it!

At the same time, however, I studied the origins and history of Buddhism. There I found myself enamored with the rich heritage and diversity within that tradition of texts, teachings, and practices. Eventually, I realized that I was operating with a double standard. While I viewed Buddhist history through a generous and charitable lens, I viewed my own religious tradition with suspicion and cynicism. This awareness challenged me to reengage Christian history with more openness.

And so I came to seminary and to Roberta Bondi.

Bondi co-taught "Introduction to Christian History," which I took during my first semester. She knew more ancient languages than God and could parse the minutest philosophical distinctions about Christ's humanity and divinity, but in that class her primary goal was to teach us one thing: to honor our mothers and fathers in the faith. Whenever it was her day to lecture, Bondi would have us sing to the mother or father we would be discussing: "Give us that old-time religion. Give us that old-time religion. Give us that old-time religion. It's good enough for us. It was good enough for _____. It was good enough for _____. It was good enough for _____. It's good enough for us." We would fill those blanks with a host of names as the weeks progressed. It was good enough for Perpetua. It was good enough for Origen. It was good enough for Benedict. It was good enough for Julian of Norwich. It was good enough for us.

Most seminary students do not come to the study of Christian history with this narrative. Indeed, most students come with little to no interest in history at all. (Why do we need a class when we have Google and Wikipedia?) But I believe this tension between history as problem and history as tradition lies at the heart of what it means to think historically about Christianity and theology. The past is problematic, and we must not be naïve about the complexity, inconsistencies, and plurality that it presents to us. Yet the past is also *our* past, the source of our Christian language and beliefs that we have received from our mothers and fathers in the faith. Thinking historically means holding these two dimensions in tension. When we do so, we are able to appropriate responsibly the theological resources of the past while also cultivating a pastoral disposition of charitable empathy. Thus, I suggest, thinking historically helps form both the mind and the heart of the theological student.

To understand what I mean, imagine an old wooden chest that has been in your family for generations. It may sit untouched, covered in cobwebs in a dusty attic corner. It may lie at the foot of your bed and hold your favorite quilts. Termites might infest it or children might play in it. In what follows, we will unpack this image of the old wooden chest in order to show how it contains traditions and problems, theological creativity and pastoral formation.

Tradition

Tradition is sometimes a dirty word for Christians. For some of us, tradition means nothing more than "the way things have always been done in our church" (where *church* means this specific building). "We have to hand out carnations on Mother's Day. It's tradition!" "We have Communion only on the first Sunday of the month. It's just tradition." But we may also see tradition as something life-giving, as a vital source for our faith that draws upon the wisdom of our communal past.

The word *tradition* comes from the Latin verb *tradere*, which means "to hand over." When we see Christian history as tradition, we acknowledge that we have received our faith from those who came before us. This does not negate the personal nature of faith and religious experience. Instead, it recognizes that the words we use, the rituals we perform, and the Scripture we read have been passed down to us like sacred family heirlooms.

Here, we see the Christian past as the old wooden chest bequeathed to us by our ancestors. The primary characteristic of this chest in this instance is its *givenness*. We did not create it. It is something we have received, whether we are aware of it or not. As children growing up in a house, we may see this piece of furniture as part of daily life. We may play with it, stub our toe on it, or store our toys in it. But we may not give it much thought. It is just there; we take it for granted.

In one important sense, this is what tradition is. Whether we recognize it or not, the Christian past shapes our present through the language, texts, and practices we have received. Part of thinking historically is simply acknowledging this fact. With so much emphasis paid to our personal experience of God or the individual use of reason, it is sobering to remember that we did not build our own Christian faith from scratch.

When we recognize the givenness of our faith, we can then experience it in new depth. Because they have been handed down to us, the vocabulary and rituals of our faith carry the past within them. Think about the old wooden chest. When we were children, it was just *there*. But as we grow older, we hear the stories about our grandparents who packed all their earthly belongings into it and hauled it onto a steamship for a long journey across the ocean. Suddenly, the chest is more than a dusty old box. It bears with it the old homeland, the hopes and fears of migration, all that was left behind and all that lay ahead.

Thinking historically about the past as tradition means recognizing the rich heritage our language and practices bear within them. For instance, consider the Nicene Creed. Although many Christians recite it in worship on a regular basis (or have it sitting unnoticed in the back of their hymnals), the creed's significance derives from its historical context. We can trace every line of the creed to a theological debate within the church. The seemingly mundane line about God the Father being the "maker of all things visible and invisible," for example, speaks to a time when Christians debated whether or not this world, with so much suffering in it, could be the product of a good and just God. What most Christians take as a fundamental element of our faith—that God created the world—was at one point a contested issue in the church. Reciting the Nicene Creed with this in mind opens us up to the significance of the claim in a new way. Just as the wooden chest becomes priceless in light of our grandparents' journey, so our Christian rituals may become sacred when we embrace the traditions they bear.

Problem

But what if our granny's story doesn't check out? What if that old wooden chest actually came from Ikea, complete with a distressed finish to give the illusion of age and experience? What if Granddad actually stole that trunk from someone else's grandparents, who never recovered from the crime? What if only part of the trunk is original and all the metal fixtures are recent additions, cobbled together from other pieces?

The critical study of history poses similar questions to our vision of the past as tradition.

Honest historical thinking recognizes that there is no such thing as a singular tradition. There are many traditions with conflicting histories for a multitude of competing Christianities. To speak of tradition only in the saccharine tones I use above can perpetuate the illusion that history is nonproblematic, objectively stable, and morally neutral. We must acknowledge that constructing a tradition can be a violent act that silences the voices of those deemed unimportant or outside the mainstream. Moreover, when we call history "tradition," we risk spackling over the holes that separate one historical moment from another, giving the illusion of an unbroken line of development.

In short, the Christian past is a problem. Thinking historically requires that we engage the sometimes difficult and uncomfortable nature of that problem in order to glean a more honest picture of Christian history.

For instance, the Christian past is not always pretty. It includes theological infighting, the Crusades, the Inquisition, collusion with colonial powers, ideological support for slavery and misogyny, and a host of other unpleasant realities.[1] Thinking historically means accepting the challenge to face these issues head-on. For some students, this means rejecting the idea of the past as tradition in any meaningful or positive sense. If earlier Christians could be so repugnant, they reason, then we must look elsewhere for our authority. This is one reason that the appeals to Scripture alone or to the historical Jesus are so popular and powerful.

Similarly, we must come to see that a multitude of different histories make up the complex story of Christianity. An earlier generation of Christians could tell themselves a comforting narrative about the one great, unbroken tradition of teaching and practice that stretched from Jesus and the apostles to their own community. Such a story provides confidence in one's own Christianity as well as a sense of superiority toward other sects who have obviously deviated from such a clear historical path. In the last few centuries, however, the academic study of history has destabilized this traditional narrative. We now must admit that Christianity has not always been the same, that it has changed drastically over time and in different cultural contexts, and that there has never been a single, universal form of faith and practice. As we note the changes and diversity within the

---

1. Denis Janz, ed., *A People's History of Christianity*, 7 vols. (Minneapolis: Fortress, 2005–2010) offers a host of essays examining many of these topics as they affected the lives of everyday Christians.

Christian past, we see how each manifestation of Christianity reflects the culture within which it arises.

How are we to think about this complex historical reality? Again, some have used this as a reason to dismiss any notion of tradition (or of "true" Christianity in general). If there is no consistency, how can we trust that what has been handed on to us is true or trustworthy? What about all the would-be traditions that have been suppressed? If our theologies and rituals are so culturally contingent, how can they ever be faithful bearers of the gospel?

Such skepticism defined my attitude toward Christian history when I started studying religion in college. When I began to reengage the past as tradition, however, I did not forget or ignore the problems of the past. Rather, I discovered new ways of thinking about the problems. For example, the messiness of the Christian past reminds us of the messiness of our fallen world in general. We too are imperfect and broken, and being able to acknowledge that brokenness in our past and our present may provide the proper disposition for understanding the possibilities of our future. Similarly, the diversity within Christian history can provide a liberating approach to tradition because it offers a wider range of authoritative options to draw upon. We may find ourselves within a particular tradition, a particular way of telling the story of Christian history, but we can claim theological resources outside that tradition as well. Learning to negotiate the plurality of the past is a large part of what it means to think historically.

Finally, thinking historically about contextualized Christianity means reflecting on the ways in which God might work in the midst of particularity—even our own. This is the ultimate payoff for thinking historically about the Christian past as a problem: recognizing ourselves as historical Christians equally shaped by the contingencies of our own contexts. If we wholly reject our problematic and pluralistic Christian past, we run the risk of presuming that we are free from those same limitations, that we alone are able to embody the *true* Christianity, to uncover the *true* Jesus, to bring about the *true* kingdom. This is not enlightenment; it is hubris.

Theological Creativity

We can spend a great deal of time thinking *about* our old wooden chest. We can admire the beauty of Nana's story while poking our heads through the holes in the plot. We can track down the forest from which the original wood was hewn and wonder how many other trunks have come from those same trees. But in the end, the chest is meant to be *used*.

There are, of course, a host of options for how to employ this problematic heirloom. Some of us might decide to restore it to its original condition and hermetically seal it to prevent any erosion. But we may also take the chest, sand it down, refinish it, and repaint it, making it more suitable for our more colorful décor. We might use it to hold new things. We might one day discover that our kids have carved their initials into it. We might even break down the components of the chest in order to incorporate them into a new piece of furniture.

In the same way, we can move beyond thinking *about* Christian history and begin thinking *with* it. When we begin to reconcile the past as tradition with the past as problem, we can begin to engage our mothers and fathers in the faith as conversation partners in all their imperfect complexity. And our options look very similar to those we have with the old wooden chest. For example, we too can be tempted to restore and seal the tradition in its original condition, striving to keep the church just as it was in some putatively pristine past. But we may also reimagine the tradition in a new context, add our experiences to it, and even fix what we see as weak spots in its design.

Of course, to do all this responsibly, we have to be intimately familiar with what we have been given. We must know the path of the wood grain and the creak of every hinge. In taking time to learn about our Christian past, we must be open to the strange wisdom it has to offer. Only then can we faithfully and fruitfully adopt and adapt it in our own lives.

With this in mind, I want to suggest three general ways we can think with our history. First, we may see historical expressions of Christianity as resources for thinking about particular contemporary problems, be they theological, pastoral, or social. For instance, modern liturgical conversations have been enriched by engagement with ancient witnesses to early forms of worship, such as the second-century writings of Justin Martyr. The fruit of this engagement has included a richer understanding of the ways Baptism and Eucharist form and sustain communal identity.[2] The general assumption of such approaches is that we need not reinvent the Christian wheel. Many of our problems are not new, and though we likely do not want to appropriate the old answers wholesale, historical expressions of the issue can help us work through our own particular assumptions and concerns about a problem.

This leads directly to the second way of thinking with our history. When we turn to historical sources as conversation partners in our own theology or ministry, we expand the boundaries of our own conceptual framework. What does this mean? Think of it this way: when we think of the past purely as tradition, we see how we have

2. See Gordon Lathrop, *Central Things: Worship in Word and Sacrament* (Minneapolis: Augsburg Fortress, 2010); Paul F. Bradshaw, *Reconstructing Early Christian Worship* (Collegeville, MN: Liturgical Press, 2009); and Don E. Saliers, *Worship as Theology: Foretaste of Glory Divine* (Nashville: Abingdon, 1994).

received theological expressions like *grace* or *sin* as well as rituals like the Lord's Supper or hymn singing. When we look at the past as a problem, though, we realize that these terms and practices are not consistent over time or between cultures. When we think *with* this complex past, we can affirm both of these realities in a constructive manner. By engaging alternative understandings of grace and sin, bread and wine, singing and praying, we expand our own theological options. A theological term that previously may have had only one flat meaning for us now has a deep and wide semantic range from which to draw. We have seen this in the recent resurgence of interest in the doctrine of the Trinity.[3] This has spurred a renewed focus on the fourth-century debates over the relationship between Father, Son, and Holy Spirit as a way to uncover the deep and diverse significance of traditional language about the triune God. By thinking with the past, we expand our own theological imagination.

This in turn contributes to the third way of thinking with Christian history. When our theological imaginations expand, we are able to perceive different ways of being Christian and of conceiving the world around us. This, I think, is the ultimate goal of thinking with our history. We are no longer bound only to our particular, limited version of Christianity. We can see that Christianity presents a wide range of faithful options for us to explore. These options include different ways of being in the world, both as individuals and as a community. For instance, the New Monasticism movement looks to ancient forms of community and hospitality as inspiration for a new way of living as Christians in a disconnected, materialistic society.[4] New Monasticism is not, however, an attempt to replicate the past. Instead, it uses the classical model of monasticism as a

---

3. See Lewis Ayres, *Nicaea and Its Legacy: An Approach to Fourth-Century Trinitarian Theology* (Oxford: Oxford University Press, 2004); and Sarah Coakley, *God, Sexuality, and the Self: An Essay 'On the Trinity'* (Cambridge: Cambridge University Press, 2013).

creative jumping-off point for imagining ways of embracing similar radical values—such as common life and contemplative spirituality—within a new context. When we think *with* the past—and not just *about* it—we draw upon the wisdom (and sometimes the folly) of the past, in all its messy otherness, in order to reimagine our present and future as Christians.

Pastoral Formation

As anyone who has taken on a project like refinishing a wooden chest knows, you cannot accomplish such a task without a few changes in yourself along the way. In my case, I am still discovering places where the cherry stain left marks on my skin that have yet to come off. I am convinced that my eyesight has been slightly damaged from staring a bit too intently at the path of the wood grain. And my decision to sand it by hand has left a permanent crick in my back. Being attentive to something precious has an effect on who you are and how you attend to other things.

Thinking historically, when done properly, also changes who we are and how we engage the world around us. To do the type of historical work I have been describing, we must develop a certain type of character, a certain moral disposition toward the past. Paul Rorem has described this aspect of historical thinking as "empathy and evaluation."[5] While I believe Rorem is correct that this pair should go together, I have found empathy to be of more dire necessity. In my experience, students are all too ready to evaluate: "This text does not quote enough Scripture." "That ancient author

---

4. For an introduction to this movement, see Jonathan Wilson-Hartgrove, *New Monasticism: What It Has to Say to Today's Church* (Grand Rapids: Brazos, 2008); and the Rutba House, eds., *School(s) for Conversion: 12 Marks of a New Monasticism* (Eugene, OR: Wipf and Stock, 2005).
5. Paul Rorem, "Empathy and Evaluation in Medieval Church History and Pastoral Ministry: A Lutheran Reading of Pseudo-Dionysius," *Princeton Seminary Bulletin* 19, no. 2 (1998): 99–115.

does not have a sufficiently modern style of exegesis." "This understanding of Jesus is too ___." "Were these people crazy?" And so on.

For this reason, when I assign papers in my introductory history courses, I instruct students not to offer their own theological opinions on the topic. They are not to say whether they agree or disagree with the historical authors. This may seem contrary to the nature of most seminary classes. After all, are we not training students to develop *their* theological voices? We certainly are, but a crucial part of developing one's own voice is learning to listen—patiently and attentively—to the voices of others.

Reading church history is slow work. It is slow because the language is strange, even when it has been translated into English. The theological worldviews of historical Christians are vastly different from ours. They had different commitments, assumptions, and symbolic tools. Most students encountering such texts for the first time are left baffled by the alien otherness of these writings. This otherness tempts us to glaze over the words as fast as we can in order to get to the end of the assignment. But such cursory reading provides little understanding of the text or those who wrote it or the Christianity they embodied. Such facile reading does not cultivate empathy.

Neither does a morally superior reaction to what we find in our Christian past. We recoil in horror at the lengths earlier Christians went to ensure doctrinal uniformity. We are baffled by their concern for what seem like abstract philosophical minutiae instead of what we know as "real" faith. We are downright offended by their uncritical and ahistorical interpretations of Scripture. But this is not thinking historically.

To approach the past with empathy is to engage it with patience and openness in order to understand it (as much as possible) on its own terms, even when we might not agree with it. Studying Christian history cultivates this disposition as we learn to linger with a text or an author or a piece of art. This patience only comes with practice. It is a discipline whose practice nurtures a virtue, a habitual way of engaging not just the past but the present as well.

Pastoral formation must also include the cultivation of empathy. A pastor entering a new congregation must be able to attend to the community and its context, to see the patterns and feel the rhythms of its life. Only then can she truly engage that congregation honestly and fruitfully. Similarly, a pastor must be able to hear the concerns of a parishioner who has come to her for counseling or with a complaint in order to understand who that person is, what he cares about, and what he desires and needs. The work of ministry requires openness to the otherness of our neighbor. We must develop an appreciation for how others view the world, how others understand the church, how others approach their faith, and even how others see us. This can only occur through a disposition of patience and openness, a disposition that historical thinking helps shape.

Perhaps what is most significant, this same empathy can allow us to understand those Christians with whom we do not agree. Too often in the religious culture wars, we only engage with straw men, cartoonish caricatures of conservatives or liberals. But in doing so we exacerbate our conflicts, because we forget that these are actual people with their own theological culture, assumptions, methods, commitments, and concerns—just like us. The work of historical thinking that I have been describing reshapes our minds and hearts to be able to empathize with the theological stranger. This does not mean we will agree with them. It means we might better appreciate and more honestly engage their Christianity after being trained to understand a wide range of historical Christianities.

After all, *those Christians* (you know, the ones *we* think are crazy), they too have a tradition. They too have inherited an old wooden chest from their mothers and fathers in the faith. They too have accepted the responsibility to preserve, care for, and pass on that sacred heirloom. Recognizing this is the first level of theological empathy. But there is also a deeper level of empathy that thinking historically provides. When we are truly attentive, we may look from our wooden chest to theirs, the two so different in color and shape, and for the first time notice the initials carved on the back of them both, the same letters in the same shaky scrawl. And then we might begin to discover what we share in our common tradition.

The End of History (or at Least of This Essay)

When I came to seminary and Roberta Bondi taught me to sing the praises of "that old-time religion" in honor of our mothers and fathers in the faith, I was just beginning to reconsider the possibility that the past could be a tradition and not just a problem. You who are reading this essay may be in a completely different place. You may be firmly committed to a critical analysis of the past, or you may be enamored with the stories of martyrs and monks. Most likely, you have no real feelings about it one way or another, except as it pertains to your course load. I am certain, however, that the baggage you bring with you includes an old wooden chest of some sort, even if you are not aware of it. Whether you were reared in a particular church or have only recently taken an interest in Christianity, you have inherited, from any number of sources, a language about faith, Scripture, and religious practices. This bequest can be both a gift and a problem, a source of life and of limitation. Because of this, it invites your attentive study and thoughtful reflection. By thinking about and with the Christian past, you will deepen your understanding not only of what Christianity is but also of who you are. Thinking historically is thus both an intellectual and a spiritual discipline. By expanding our theological imagination and cultivating the virtue of empathy, engaging the past helps shape who we will be as Christians in the future.

6

Thinking Systematically

Amy Marga

There are no bystanders to God's self-revelation.

This is the first premise of thinking systematically. Those who feel compelled to begin the intense journey of talking about God in a coherent and rational way do so because they have experienced the living God. This divine presence in Jesus Christ through the Holy Spirit is so free, so undomesticated, so challenging that the people who encounter it have no choice but to work to make sense out of such an experience. They know that something happened.

To be encountered by this one is to experience a new sense of yourself, your place in the world, and your priorities. God's self-revelation beckons all believers to become theologians. Theologians join an ongoing conversation about God's love and grace in the world; it is a conversation that has been going on for centuries, throughout human cultures. It demands listening. It calls for action. It clings to the prayer "Come, Holy Spirit."

Anselm, the twelfth-century bishop of Canterbury, defined thinking systematically as *faith seeking understanding*. His words insist that thinking systematically is about *God*. In other words, it can happen only from the perspective of faith. Thinking systematically is not study of the phenomena of human religiosity or a psychology of religion. It is not a sociological study of a community's religious practices.

Rather, thinking systematically about God is the work of organizing one's experience of God as a living subject among the wide variety of witnesses to God. It is the task of faith to articulate experiences of God so that they stand in a logical—even if critical—relationship to all the other witnesses to God's work.

Thinking Systematically Is Like a Journey

The process of thinking systematically about God can be described as a winding road. It is a trail of thought that treads back and forth along the desert paths of the biblical narrative. It travels the cloudy past of Christian thought passed down through the ages. It sails within the currents of contemporary human experience.

This road is often traveled with a commitment to a particular creed or confession, such as the Lutheran Confessions as compiled in the *Book of Concord* or the Episcopalian *Book of Common Prayer*.[1] These commitments carried by the theologian provide continuity, perspective, and perhaps a little comfort in the struggle to make sense of how God is working in human history today; they are the tools of the theologian.

---

1. Robert Kolb, James Schaffer, Timothy Wengert, eds., *The Book of Concord*, 2nd ed. (Minneapolis: Fortress Press, 2000) and The Episcopal Church, *Book of Common Prayer* (New York: Seabury Press, 1976).

It is no small task to decide upon reliable sources of knowledge as one thinks systematically. For instance, should modern science be a privileged conversation partner for theology today? Or, as another example, are historical texts like the Lutheran Confessions the most faithful way to interpret the biblical witness to Christ's work?

These questions are not new. The second-century theologian Justin Martyr relied upon the dominant philosophical language of his day to describe Christ as the logos of God. His contemporaries could then relate to Christ through a Greek concept that was familiar to them: the Logos as the cosmic, beautiful, rational ordering principle of the natural world.[2] When Thomas Aquinas spoke of God as the Unmoved mover, he was innovating based on the newly rediscovered texts of Aristotle that were circulating through thirteenth-century Italy.[3] In modern theological reflection, James Cone looks to the music and lyrics of American slave spirituals as voices of the Christian faith under a racist and oppressive system.[4] Much like the Psalms, these slave spirituals are a resource for systematic theological reflection.

Seeking out historical voices that illuminate the scriptural witness to God's activity for today is central to thinking systematically. Resources come in the forms of confessional creeds, prayers, songs, philosophical works, even cultural attitudes. These are the tools that theologians carry on their journey.

Finding Places to Rest on the Thought Journey of Theology

Resting places matter on this journey of faith and discovery.

2. Justin Martyr, *The First and Second Apologies*, trans. Leslie W. Barnard (New York: Paulist Press, 1997).
3. Thomas Aquinas, *Summa Contra Gentiles*, bk. 1, ch. 13, http://dhspriory.org/thomas/ContraGentiles.htm.
4. James Cone, *The Cross and the Lynching Tree* (Maryknoll, NY: Orbis Books, 2011).

The thinking theologian chooses places upon which to settle and make sense of God's activity. One might find a resting place in a particular school of thought, in the writings of a particular theologian past or present, or in a compelling conversation with a classmate or colleague. Resting places provide a home for our theologies to grow, but the best resting places don't cultivate complacency; rather, they inspire continued learning.

For centuries, the most common theological resting place has been the European or Mediterranean male experience. One reason for this is that cultures and philosophies have historically claimed that only European or Mediterranean males have had the intellectual capacity to think in a rational way about God. Women and dark-skinned men were seen as having no such capacity. Unwittingly or not, the historical record of theology mostly contains thinking done *by* men *for* men, even though from time immemorial women and people of color have been thinking rigorously and rationally about God as well.

Today, cultural and political structures have allowed more and more women to reflect publically upon God's nature and work. Theologians are resting, for instance, in the experiences of African American women. Womanist theologians like Delores Williams and Jacquelyn Grant think rigorously about God's action and the agency of black women, especially through the lens of the embodied, black, female experience.[5] Amos Yong thinks systematically about the Holy Spirit from his commitment to the Pentecostal faith.[6] White feminist thinkers such as Elizabeth Johnson have rigorously reflected on the

---

5. *Womanist* is a term coined by Alice Walker to describe social theory and philosophical thought done specifically from the perspective of black women. See Delores Williams, *Sisters in the Wilderness: The Challenge of Womanist God-Talk* (Maryknoll, NY: Orbis Books, 1993); and Jacquelyn Grant, *White Women's Christ and Black Women's Jesus: Feminist Christology and Womanist Response* (Atlanta: Scholars Press, 1989).

6. Amos Yong, *The Spirit Poured Out on All Flesh: Pentecostalism and the Possibility of Global Theology* (Grand Rapids: Baker Academic, 2005); and idem., *Spirit of Love: A Trinitarian Theology of Grace* (Waco, TX: Baylor University Press, 2012).

way human language shrinks or expands believers' imaginations about God.[7]

Theologians across the globe—from the suffering places of oppressed *dalit* groups in India to the places of poverty and liberation in Latin America and the United States[8]—are thinking systematically about what it means to have faith in God's work within and despite oppressive economic and political systems. Other resting places along the theologian's journey are found in the traumatic experiences of reproductive loss,[9] the survival of abuse,[10] or the experiences of prejudice toward those outside the norm of heterosexuality.[11] These are only some of many stops along the way.

When theologians rest among particular peoples and within particular experiences, they often can see more clearly the folly and ugliness of those who oppress, exploit, and hate. Resting places help theologians cultivate this kind of vision. They help theologians uncover their own assumptions and face the limits of their own systems of thought.

These resting places matter deeply for thinking systematically about God because God delights in encountering people in these spaces too. When theologians stand still for a while among the existential realities of particular communities, they begin to

---

7. Elizabeth Johnson, *She Who Is: The Mystery of God in Feminist Theological Discourse* (New York: Crossroad, 1992).

8. Peniel Rajkumar, *Dalit Theology and Dalit Liberation: Problems, Paradigms, and Possibilities* (Surrey: Ashgate, 2010); Gustavo Gutiérrez, *A Theology of Liberation: History, Politics, and Salvation* (Maryknoll, NY: Orbis Books, 1973); and Miguel De La Torre, *Handbook on U.S. Theologies of Liberation* (St. Louis: Chalice Press, 2004).

9. Serene Jones, *Trauma and Grace: Theology in a Ruptured World* (Louisville, KY: Westminster John Knox Press, 2009).

10. Rita Brock and Rebecca Parker, *Proverbs of Ashes: Violence, Redemptive Suffering and the Search for What Saves Us* (Boston: Beacon Press, 2001).

11. See as only one example, Gerard Loughlin, ed., *Queer Theology: Rethinking the Western Body* (Malden, MA: Blackwell, 2007).

comprehend how it pleases God to move and work among those who have traditionally been voiceless, despised, or forgotten.

Theological reflections from such a variety of perspectives uncover God's hidden works within the secular veils of human history. In these places, believers see the way that God's works of love create strength, foster resilience, and encourage laughter among believers. Indeed, resting places matter on the thought journey of systematic theology.

The Use of Human Cognitive Powers in Thinking Systematically

Systematic theology requires thinking Christians to utilize all their powers of sensing, knowing, and experiencing the world in order to make sense of God's activity.

John Wesley, the founder of Methodism, named these human powers within a "quadrilateral" of Scripture, tradition, experience, and reason. Using Scripture, experience, reason, and tradition, believers tell the stories of God's work in their lives and in the world in ways that are logical and rational. This is thinking systematically. It sets out to make claims about God's nature that are based on the narrative of God's work in Scripture and based on God's work in people's lives.

For instance, the Gospel of Mark is one way that a community set out to tell the narrative of God's work. The Gospel of Mark is hardly a systematic theology in that it does not try to follow certain rules of logic. Nor is it giving the reader a set of propositions that require assent in order for the reader to be properly faithful. However, it does give a coherent narrative of God's work in Christ that takes into account life events, places, persons, and cultural realities that resonated in and were central to the community of which Mark was a part. This narrative forms the basis for further reflection about God.

Thinking systematically takes the narratives of God's activity and the narratives of people's lives seriously. It seeks to give an account of God's love for humanity in ways that are compelling and convincing to those seeking to understand the nature of their experience of God's revelation.

Relevancy and Authority in Thinking Systematically

Systematic expressions of God inevitably deal with issues of authority and relevance. For some theologians, the *relevancy* of God's word happens when believers obey the *authoritative* words of Christian leaders and adhere to Christian teaching through their lifestyles and attitudes. For others, by contrast, the *authority* of God's word is felt only when that word pierces the din of secular life and touches the listener in a highly *relevant* way.

Systematic theologians who prioritize authority over relevancy emphasize the correctness and precision of Christian teachings. They often see themselves doing dogmatic or systematic theology because their theological reflections form the basis for official church teachings. They base theology's authority on the premise that theological expression is an elongation of God's own word through Jesus Christ. Roman Catholic dogmatic theology is an example of an authoritative approach. Following the thought of Thomas Aquinas, it sets up doctrine as the authority over believers' lives and faith practices. Theology is literally sacred doctrine in the Roman Catholic Church.[12]

Another example of authoritative theology can be found in various communities within American evangelicalism. The preaching and

---

12. Thomas Aquinas, *Summa Theologica*, part one, question one, http://www.ccel.org/ccel/aquinas/summa.toc.html.

views of American evangelical leaders hold a particular kind of theological authority over believers. This authority arises from their understanding of how God's word has been revealed in literal and untainted ways in the Bible. Theologians in these communities are more concerned with whether systematic expression of God aligns with authoritative sources such as church leadership, the Bible, and tradition. They hold that if believers follow the authoritative word of theology in their moral choices and lifestyles, it is relevant in people's lives.

For other theologians, such as Paul Tillich, Jürgen Moltmann, Sallie McFague, and Serene Jones, systematic thinking carries authority only when it speaks a relevant word of grace and reconciliation into people's existential realities. In these cases, authority follows from relevancy, not the other way around. Such theologians closely investigate the deep cultural and existential concerns people have and then work to express how God is active within the domestic lives and daily activities of people.

Theologians concerned with the relevancy of theology are often inclined to see themselves as doing constructive theology. Constructive reflection on God's presence requires intense curiosity about the deep needs of people in secular society. It draws deeply from a wide variety of disciplines such as history, politics, psychology, the arts, and ethics. It sees these other disciplines as probing the reality of transcendence in the same way that theology seeks to do.

If thinking systematically can arise only out of an experience of God, then no doctrine, no matter how perfectly articulated or biblically sound it might be, will form the basis of authority for our talk about God. Only God grants authority to human expression. This theological fact prevents thinking systematically from becoming the exclusive task of any one group of people. Rather, thinking systematically happens when believers face the sobering conditions of human existence, no matter if they prefer the authoritative model or the relevancy model of theology.

Systematic thinking about God becomes actual expressions of *God* only when God's own being lifts it up and uses it for God's own reconciling purposes. This is the dialectic that human speaking about God consistently finds itself in. It is eloquently expressed by Karl Barth, who says that based on human experience of God's self-revelation, we want to speak of God, indeed, we *must* speak of God. But we know that human language cannot fully capture God's free and loving spirit—we *cannot* speak of God. God remains the subject of thinking systematically, and in this truth, God is glorified.[13] God chooses which of our words and our thoughts express God's love and power. Unless God chooses to imbue our thinking with God's spirit, then it will lack both authority and relevancy.

There Is No Such Thing as Pure Systematic Thinking about a Living Subject

Because only God can make systematic thinking relevant and authoritative, theologians must continually face the truth that they are dealing with a divine, living subject. Despite the human desire to capture and bottle (and sell) that which is beautiful, loving, and good, God refuses to be captured. God is never satisfied to be an object of human reason or imagination. God as the eternal subject comes to humanity in ways that often confound the mind and overturn established notions of power and logic. This is seen nowhere more

---

13. "As theologians, we ought to speak of God. But we are humans and as such cannot speak of God. We ought to do both, to know the 'ought' and the 'not able to,' and precisely in this way give God the glory." Karl Barth, "The Word of God as the Task of Theology," in *The Word of God and Theology*, trans. Amy Marga, T&T Clark Studies in Systematic Theology (New York: Bloomsbury, 2011), 177.

clearly than in the revelation of God's very being in the newborn baby, Jesus Christ, found at the breast of his mother, Mary.

And perhaps the absurdity and unexpectedness of a young mom and her baby or the man executed on a cross is precisely the manner in which God reminds us that the mortal mind can never dictate the boundaries of God's love and reconciling work. Perhaps the deepest insight gained by thinking systematically about God is realizing that the infinitely loving and living God can never be captured as a system at all! In this way, the term *systematic theology* exists as a paradox, for its work depends upon the living subject who is God.

The more one studies the Bible and human history, the more one gets the sense that the living God is never satisfied to settle into our expressions of doctrine or any other kind of human system. Systematic theology can hardly be a system in the sense that each part is tightly bound to the whole through some kind of logic or foundation, the way, say, computer code is written or the way lower math operates by certain unshakeable rules. God does not utilize any philosophical or scientific foundation to reveal God's being in the world.

Instead, thinking systematically is thinking *from* and *with* the living God. Thinking systematically gives the theologian over to the rush of God's loving and free revelation. It is the continuous movement of the mind that follows after the surprising, mysterious movement of the living God. God's movement within history is sometimes as clear as the crying child to whom we effortlessly open our arms. Sometimes it is as fluid and indefinite as the reflection of the moon in water. This is the exhilaration of thinking systematically. It is making sense out of the living God.

Thinking Systematically about God the Living Subject is Practical

Because systematic thinking seeks to follow the movement of the living God, it can be said that thinking systematically is a profoundly practical activity. It is as much about *listening, acting* and *praying* as it is about *thinking*. Indeed, we are crossing boundaries of academic disciplines when we make such a statement. The lines of constructive theology and practical theology are beginning to blur in the twenty-first century. Whether one calls oneself a constructive or dogmatic or practical theologian, thinking systematically about God is an activity in which all believers—no matter their academic pedigree—can and do engage because of their daily encounters with the living God.

The practical task of systematic theology has been recognized through the ages. Thinkers like Augustine of Hippo valued the orderly presentation of Christian teaching as a path toward wisdom.[14] Thomas Aquinas believed that the church could help people live godly lives through its orderly presentation of teachings about God's work. Modern and postmodern theologians seek a more godly existence through the deconstruction of oppressive political and linguistic systems in a globally connected world. In order to be true to this practical task, systematic theology must listen, act, and pray.

Listening Comes before Thinking

Listening is a practice that helps the theologian see and understand God's beloved world. People who think systematically can do so only out of the practice of listening closely to the needs of their communities. They listen to the ways that culture and language shape

---

14. Augustine, *De doctrina Christiana*, trans. and ed. R. P. H. Green (Oxford: Clarendon Press, 1995). See also Ellen Charry, *By the Renewing of Your Minds: The Pastoral Function of Christian Doctrine* (New York: Oxford University Press, 1997).

people's thoughts about existence and reality.[15] They cultivate an ear for the natural world. They hold on to people's expressions of God's love. They mourn with others about the suffering that leaves no human untouched. The ear of the theologian is deep. It takes in the human desire for communion with God.

Today, listening deeply for the sake of thinking systematically also requires trust in the perspectives and ideas of a wide variety of people who are trying to make sense of God's revelation. Listening to the voices of black women who experience God's presence in the struggles of family means the theologian trusts that their experiences reflect reality. Listening to Latina women express their struggles under unjust working conditions means acknowledging that their experiences matter to God and to us.[16] Listening to young people today talk about their nonaffiliation with traditional church bodies means respecting that they too are working to make sense out of their experiences of the world and of God's work in it.[17]

Listening thus moves into the practice of *seeing* those for whom life is a struggle or who live on the margins of dominant cultural groups. Listening moves into seeing, the way God saw Hagar with her son Ishmael, desperate in the wilderness.[18] Systematic theology is an honest intellectual discipline when it listens to and sees the way people participate in God's ongoing revelation and activity in the world. But it cannot stop there. The theologian must listen and act.

15. Paul Tillich made it a priority in his theology to listen to culture for theology. See his *Systematic Theology*, vol. 1 (Chicago: University Of Chicago Press, 1973).
16. Ada María Isasi-Díaz, *Mujerista Theology: A Theology for the Twenty-first Century* (Maryknoll, NY: Orbis Books, 1996).
17. See for example, the sociological study by Christian Smith, *Souls in Transition: The Religious and Spiritual Lives of Emerging Adults* (Oxford: Oxford University Press, 2009).
18. Genesis 16 and 21.

Action Comes before Thinking

Acting is the second practice of thinking systematically. Theologians listen, see, and act, but maybe not in this order. Sometimes acting on behalf of others out of one's faith in God can lead to truly seeing and thinking systematically about how God works among particular communities. That is, sometimes we have to move in faith, to act, only then to discover someone to whom we must listen intently.

Such action might take the shape of preaching or teaching within believing communities. It might take place in a missional way among those who have not yet heard the good news of Jesus Christ, or it might take the form of political action and a fight for the justice that Christ's death has promised everyone. It might take shape through the intimate relationships of family and home. It often happens among those who are invisible in the dominant culture. However it happens, one can think systematically about God's nature only out of a life of action. The power of such praxis–oriented systematic thinking can be seen in a theologian like Gustavo Gutiérrez, a Roman Catholic priest in Peru. In the 1960s, he witnessed the extreme poverty of the people in his neighborhood and decided to *act* as a Christian and as a theologian. Out of his acts of care for the poor, he reflected and thought systematically about what it means that God not only loves the poor but also prefers to be found among the poor.[19]

Beware: action with and for others requires courage. It is a risk! Many theologians are not comfortable being risk takers. They like to observe. But systematic theology has no room for mere commentators, because there are no mere onlookers to God's self-revelation. The living God pulls the thinker along into risk, into the exigencies of human life, into a future that is not yet clear.

19. Gustavo Gutiérrez, *A Theology of Liberation: History, Politics and Salvation* (Maryknoll, NY: Orbis Books, 1973).

Such a risk cost the life of Oscar Romero, a priest from El Salvador who spoke out against political oppression. He was assassinated while performing a Catholic Mass. It also cost the life of German Lutheran theologian Dietrich Bonhoeffer, executed for his involvement in a plot to assassinate Hitler. A theologian plotting an assassination of a dictator: this is the action and the risk that thinking systematically may entail.

Thinking Depends on the Prayer "Come, Holy Spirit"

We can talk about thinking, listening, and acting for a long time. But if the theologian does not finally pray for the presence and the power of the Holy Spirit, theology is nothing but a pile of unnecessary words. The most faithful position of the systematic theologian is not standing behind a lecture podium or hunched over a writing desk or even engaging "the world" through social media. It is the position of prayer. People who think systematically can do only one thing to make their activity legitimate.

Pray.

This is the ultimate and indispensable practice of the theologian. The most important words that can come out of the theologian's mouth are "Come, Holy Spirit," because it is a prayer asking God to take up all the talking and acting and use it as God sees fit. Theologians pray, "Come Holy Spirit," for they know that in the end all human speaking of God is speaking of a being who exceeds any and all human conception of love, faithfulness, goodness, and justice. The systematic theologian is at her best when she is in prayer before God.

In listening, acting, and praying, the systematic theologian is not working toward some kind of correct articulation of God's nature. Rather, the theologian works to express the living God's activity in ways that are faithful to the scriptural witness and in ways that make sense to both believers and nonbelievers. Thinking systematically is not about lording religious or moral authority over any other believer based on the status of the theologian as a person.

Systematic theology is about offering one's rational thoughts, wisdom, imagination, words, and actions to God for God's own use for the sake of our neighbors. Giving the working of our minds up to God's gracious will demonstrates that the priority of thinking systematically is being able to have a loving and saving effect on the one listening or reading. Its task is to help believers become wise about the vagaries of human life and confident in the unending faithfulness of God. Within the struggles of human existence, it shines a light upon the new beginnings God makes with God's beloved humanity.

Surely, what has been laid out here is no small task for the one who desires to think systematically about the nature of God. All believers think systematically on some level, because all believers are working to make sense of their lives and God's work in them. Systematic theologians can help people embrace the human capacity to listen, act, and pray. Within the mosaic of human fullness, believers make sense of God's reconciling, loving work for them and for others. When thinking systematically about God brings forth reconciliation and new creation, systematic theologians have done their job.

7

Thinking Ethically

Matilde Moros

What does it mean to think ethically, from a Christian perspective? The answer is complicated and nuanced and often leaves people looking for a quick and easy list of guidelines. I have been teaching Christian ethics to seminary students for a few years now. Almost without exception, each time I introduce students to the study of ethics, they seem most interested in obtaining a list of precise rules and a clear description of what a good Christian is like. The list they are requesting is a morally binding, "what not to do" catalog, a concise set of guidelines by which to live a life that stays on the good side of God. In short, they are waiting for me to tell them that Christian ethics boils down to an individual's morals. A student will ask if we are going to study the Ten Commandments or if we will go to the book of Proverbs for guidance. Though we do study these texts in deep and meaningful ways, they are not really lists of nos and don'ts, cannots and must nots. And so I tend to respond with a pastoral and rhetorical question. Instead of answering the questions directly, I ask different questions. I ask and organize us to work collectively, as the theologians and ethicists that we each are, to answer the base questions: What do we mean by Christian ethics, and specifically what does it mean to do Christian social ethics? In the end, Christian ethics is nothing less than a study and embodiment of those practices that will lead us to love God and neighbor and so participate in God's transformation of the world.

Where Do We Start?

To unpack years of prescribed images and lists of what good and evil are means that we first take a step back and look at how this understanding of ethics came into our current imagination. What has changed in our reading of Scripture, traditions, histories, and theologies, and at the same time how have Christians interpreted these changing elements that are crucial to understanding ethics?

To assist with this unpacking, textbooks on Christian ethics, with perspectives ranging from historical to methodological, have been helpful to my students. For example, J. Philip Wogaman makes it clear that the Bible, as a source for Christian ethics, must be understood as a book with many theologies and many ethics in it.[1] So, how does any Christian learn to think ethically? How do students in seminary think ethically as a theological practice? What binds Christians together so that they might think ethically about the world around them? While many would point out that Scripture itself binds us ecumenically, we also know that the history, translation, and interpretation of this sacred text are incredibly complex. So, if we are not trained biblical scholars, how do we read and understand Scripture in a way that gives us ethical insight?

---

1. J. Phillip Wogaman, *Christian Ethics: A Historical Introduction* (Louisville, KY: Westminster John Knox, 1993).

First and foremost, we do not pick and choose parts of Scripture to make our point or to rationalize our understanding of Christian moral or ethical behavior. Rather, we discern and pray and gather as much information as possible. And even as we discern and pray and think, we must remember that even Christians who have dedicated themselves to the study of the Bible have done terrible things in the name of Christ. And so thinking ethically is as much about the study of our present challenges as it is about our past, whether good or ill.

Doing Ethics

To do ethics from a biblical perspective means that we must acknowledge certain tensions in Scripture. These tensions include philosophical and contextual influences as well as theological developments, schisms, and divides that have affected how we understand Scripture. Beyond these in history and theology, we can add the diversity of cultural, social, and political contexts in which people, places, and ideas have shaped who we are as Christians in the twenty-first century. How then are we to understand who we are and how we should live? How do we strive for unity in the midst of so much difference?

One approach to Christian ethics utilizes the methods developed by philosophical ethicists; here Western philosophy has influenced Christian ethics most directly. The unification of Christian thought under the guise of Western philosophy, however, does not always take into account the variety of peoples and philosophies we find in the vast history of Christianity. This diversity must be part of our understanding of how doctrine has developed and shaped Christian communities and how theological differences have emerged.

Sometimes, the ethical response to a dominant view of Christian hegemonic unity is to work ecumenically and take difference into account. That is, we start with a diversity of approaches not from any one dogmatic theological or philosophical understanding. A moral or ethical Christian framework that takes variation into account must begin with a robust historical understanding and point to a future that from the present time and place can state what *ought or should be*. In contrast, ethical reasoning from a Western philosophical perspective tends to work from a sense of "objectivity." However, to think objectively is itself problematic. Instead of relying exclusively on the Western philosophical tradition's influence on Christian ethics, I teach that to think theologically and ethically one must think of historical particularities. Instead of supposedly universal and objective conclusions, I invite my students to discover the ethical wisdom found in particular peoples and communities, especially in their complex histories and cultures.

The Western philosophical tradition is but one of many influences on Christian ethics. It cannot claim to be an exclusive or a flawless source for Christian ethics. The Western philosophical tradition is both valuable and limited. And so we place these traditions in conversation with other communities of thought. Christian ethics, therefore, is not exclusively determined by the ways Western philosophers have traditionally thought about ethics. Rather, Christian ethicists follow the "way" that Jesus of Nazareth taught his followers, a way characterized by its inclusion of the poorest and most excluded into the fold of the community. At core, Jesus' life and teachings proclaimed and lived out justice and the radical transformation of the world. Ethical discernment thus becomes the discovery of what it means to be a people in the realm or kingdom of God. In short, Christian ethics wonders how exactly we love God and neighbor.

The injunction to love recurs regularly in the Gospels.[2] Starting with this command, we can develop a theology and ethic that moves through tolerance to justice for those who have been excluded, oppressed, and despised. Jesus' parables, his teachings, his way of life, his vision and embodiment of the kingdom of God become the parameters around which we organize Christian ethics. And yet the call to love God and neighbor as self is perhaps the hardest commandment to follow. We, as Christians, continue to navigate between a world of impossibilities and the dream and promise of a new covenant, between a new world that is both now and not yet. This is the promise, a kingdom in which God dwells and rules within and among us in all righteousness.

Christian ethics then is not so easily defined. We need to find a way of looking at the world through a new paradigm, even as we continue to draw upon the lenses of Scripture, the history of Christianity, the development of doctrine and belief, and our various Christian theologies. Christian ethics in the twenty-first century is not primarily about moral codes, isolated biblical references, or the institutional reach of the church. Based on the Judeo-Christian concept of justice, Christian ethics are about values, sometimes understood through Western philosophical lenses but at other times defined by the example we have in the Gospel descriptions of Jesus' ministry: his words and deeds, his sacrifice, and his promise of the kingdom of God on earth as it is in heaven.

Righteous, love-based, Christian social ethics will need to draw from diverse voices that may just disrupt our assumptions and from marginalized voices that may just reorient our sense of justice. Through various methods like liberationist, feminist, womanist, *mujerista*, critical race, and other perspectives,[3] Christian ethics can be

2. See, for example, Matt. 22:38 as well as Lev. 19:18, Matt. 19:19, Rom. 13:8, 10, and Gal. 5:14.
3. See, respectively, Miguel De La Torre, *Doing Christian Ethics from the Margins* (Maryknoll, NY: Orbis, 2004); Lois K. Daly, *Feminist Theological Ethics: A Reader* (Louisville, KY: Westminster John Knox, 1994); Dolores S. Williams, *Sisters in the Wilderness: The Challenge of Womanist God-Talk* (Maryknoll, NY: Orbis, 1993); Ada María Isasi-Díaz, *Mujerista Theology: A Theology*

framed to embrace the realities of excluded communities. It is evident that an ethic of greed that simply disregards others is not a Christian ethic. No, this would be a self-centered ethic. In contrast, Christian ethics is an other-centered way of life, as it is centered in God first.

So how is it that we can discern how to love our neighbor as we love ourselves? Compassion, kindness, and other practices of love are ways in which we show others *our* love for them. However, the ethics of the kingdom of God are about the *action of God* in this world. If God's actions are in view, then our actions will necessarily involve risk, solidarity, and the shaping of the conscience. Action calls us to move beyond interpretation or showing or intellectual assent. Action is doing. Action is being. Action is creating new ways of embodying and practicing the righteous love of God, neighbor, and self.

Though in ethics we speak about the common good as a philosophical inheritance from the Western tradition, the common good is really a theological conviction. We believe that there is a common reality in which God and creation, God and creature are in the same household of life. The common good is one way to think ethically. It is a way to understand the kingdom of God as a reign of justice. Such a notion of the kingdom and the common good might just change the world.

Being Ethical

How do we understand this household in which God and us together dwell? More and more, Christians in a globalized world understand that the history of globalization, conquest, and colonization have always been a part of our religious history and experience. This history took an important turn for Christians with Europe's global,

for the Twenty-First Century (Maryknoll, NY: Orbis, 1996); and Traci West, *Disruptive Christian Ethics: When Racism and Women's Lives Matter* (Louisville, KY: Westminster John Knox, 2006).

imperial expansion. This expansion was conducted under the banner of Christian faith, and so the entire world was exposed to Western Christian values, whether for good or not. So ubiquitous was this expansion that we still feel its effects today; this history has shaped a common experience for the planetary household. And so ethical concerns spring from the reality that we Christians have been responsible for the creation of justice and injustice alike and so bear the obligation to be honest about our history in the contemplation and practice of an ethics of justice.

So, how do we understand these ambiguities and contradictions within our own traditions?

Often, Christian ethicists approach thinking ethically about social injustices through the theology and ethics of a particular Christian in history. That individual's ethics then serve as an example that opens up discussion about how Scripture and the particularity of one's social location, historical reality, and relationship with the world shape not only how one thinks but also how one acts in the world. Dietrich Bonhoeffer, Martin Luther King, Jr., Dorothy Day, Oscar Romero, and Thomas Merton are just a few examples of individuals who lived out of their Christian convictions and upon whose lives we can base a Christian ethic.[4] Through the examination of a particular life and the consideration of prophetic action in the world, Christians can be examples to other Christians.

For instance, while in prison awaiting execution, Dietrich Bonhoeffer wrote letters to the next generation about the meaning of

---

4. See, for example, Jürgen Moltmann and Jürgen Weissbach, *Two Studies in the Theology of Bonhoeffer*, trans. Reginald H. Fuller and Ilse Fuller (New York: Scribner, 1967); Hak Joon Lee, *We Will Get to the Promised Land: Martin Luther King, Jr.'s Communal-Political Spirituality* (Cleveland: Pilgrim, 2006); Patrick Jordan, ed., *Dorothy Day: Writings from Commonweal* (Collegeville, MN: Liturgical Press, 2002); Jose María López Vigil, *Oscar Romero: Memories in Mosaic*, trans. Kathy Ogle (Washington, DC: EPICA, 2000); and William H. Shannon, *Witness to Freedom: The Letters of Thomas Merton in Times of Crisis* (New York: Farrar, Straus, Giroux, 1994).

home. Although he was specifically speaking to the next generation in his family about their family home, his words continue to resonate across the generations. As Bonhoeffer stated, "In the revolutionary times ahead the greatest gift will be to know the security of a good home. It will be a bulwark against all dangers from within and without."[5] Though centered in a context in which history seemed doomed, this statement is perhaps also about a Christian apocalyptic understanding of Jesus' second coming as the "revolutionary times ahead." For Bonhoeffer, danger lurks both within and without our church family, our home.

We think about family in many ways. Christians often call the church their family. In other words, our kin is one way, but not the only way, we understand our common bonds. We understand that home is the place where families, communities, and individuals can thrive, rest, and grow. And home is more than the material structures of our houses. Home is God's presence. Home is a critical part of God's creation. Home is how we organize ourselves as a people. Home helps us know who our neighbor is. Home is self. Home is a body.

And that body that is our home is the resurrected body of Jesus, for the resurrection imbues our bodies with new life even now. So if we share Jesus' body, then why can't we Christians see ourselves as one? Perhaps because we tend to focus on the dangers and fears that populate this world and not on the security of home, the security of death defeated, the security of God's power above all other power. Indeed, as Bonhoeffer stated, the greatest gift we have is our security in this kingdom home, a good home, a common-good and righteous home, which is here and yet to come.

5. Dietrich Bonhoeffer, *Letters and Papers from Prison* (New York: Simon and Schuster, 1997), 295.

Thinking ethically implores us to *do* ethics and *become* ethical. It is a process by which we observe, reflect, and then act. After we act, we reflect and observe again in order to act once again. Ethics then is communal and individual, historical and contextual, God-centered and neighbor-centered, because that is how we love as Christians, both from the inside out and from the outside in. Jesus taught us that we belong to God's household. As such, thinking ethically is about household and belonging. It is about the community of God, neighbor, and self, and so it is also about making righteousness our priority.

Conditions for Thinking Ethically

Doing Christian ethics means that we respect and love our common humanity, our common creation, and our common life. To do this, we must first place our trust in the God who created us to be in relationship with one another. But what happens when we do not respect, love, or trust the other? In a broken and violent world, it is more common to find brokenness in individuals and in community than it is to see the holistic, life-abundant, and righteous promise of the kingdom of God in action. It is the violated, the hungry, the ill, the excluded, the homeless to whom is first promised the kingdom of God and its security, a security that is the gift of a good home away from danger within and throughout this world.

The vulnerability of the endangered is precisely where God reigns. It is there that we find our obligations to one another. Faith teaches us how to trust that such dire contexts are where new life is born, not because we fix the broken, rescue the imprisoned, or deliver the endangered but because God is in that place, that body, that situation. So where should Christians be when God is acting in the world? Christians should be in those broken and vulnerable places. Christians should be *acting* and *doing* our ethics as much as, if not more than, we *think about* ethics. As Christians, we strive for justice. We live into righteousness. We not only lament the state of the world, but we also trust in the "revolutionary times ahead" when God turns everything upside down. It is scriptural, it is faithful, it is the way of Jesus to put the household of God in place, so that we do not fear our brokenness but trust and love life and God's action in the world.

No list of prohibitions, not any one part of Scripture, not any one institution, not any one individual in the Christian community has all the ethical answers to what it means to be a "good" Christian. Being truly ethical and calling yourself a Christian are too often quite opposite realities. Our relationship within the household of God is doomed by dysfunction. We have ill relationships with other peoples. We have ill relationships with creation. We have ill relationships within our own Christian communities, and so the dangers within are as much of the equation as the dangers without when it comes to building a common good, which is the foundation of a good home.

The God of life, the Christ that draws us into relationship, and the loving Spirit guide us into a sense of justice that seeks to rectify these relationships gone wrong. Yet, it is God's will for us to have a will toward love. It is God's will that we too have creativity and imagination, and that we understand the poetic ways of Scripture not only as prohibitions but also as invitations to see the glory of God in the possibilities of justice and love. A peaceful household can only be the result of a reign of love in which the triad of God, neighbor, and self are all in right relationship. Thinking ethically is complicated, it is nuanced with much theology, it is a Christian obligation, but it is also a delight.

In the end, thinking ethically is not merely about being nice. Delight in God is joyous; being nice is just being nice. Polite and quiet behavior is not a safe indication of personal morality or piety.

Respecting someone's individual boundaries is not the crux of Christian values. Instead, being ethical in the Christian tradition has meant defying the status quo when injustice is involved. It has meant sometimes choosing to be "not nice," standing boldly and courageously for what is right in the midst of terrible wrong. Thinking about right relationship and common-good values is about more than any one person's individual rights.

Christian values at their best are about a whole way of being that is constructed in relationship and that is other-centered. The kingdom of God requires that we become the revolutionary times that are ahead, while creating with hope in the now a reign of God that has not yet fully arrived.

8

Thinking Socially

Stephanie Buckhanon Crowder

Cell phones and computers are the everyday companions of most of us, from the uber rich to the poor and struggling. Financial planners in China communicate with Wall Street moguls in less than a minute via text or e-mail. Students in South Africa can exchange educational ideas over video with peers in California because of the unfathomable speed of broadband and WiFi or radio signals. From hospitals to colleges, boardrooms to small huts in the middle of the desert, the span of the Internet is global and yet somehow still growing in influence

Technology is so pervasive that nothing has escaped its reach, not even the church. Facebook not only facilitates meeting new people or former acquaintances with "like" interests, but pastors also use it to market upcoming worship services and engage in crowd sourcing for sermon preparation. Instagram allows for the immediate uploading of pictures and videos from congregational gatherings and bulletins. Preachers can even offer a teaser on their upcoming sermons. Twitter, with its readily available news feeds, has become a primary means of following people and organizations to learn more about who is doing what, when, and where. One can even message or talk without dialing a phone number. The ability to market one's self, ministry, church, and programs to thousands upon tens of thousands can happen perhaps in less time than it takes to read the first few pages of this essay.

The aforementioned are just a few (and I do mean a very few) of the forms and uses of technology. Pinterest, YouTube, Flickr, LinkedIn, Digg, Tumblr (and the list goes on and on and on . . .) can take a person's message and personality to infinity and beyond. Apps abound for just about any purpose and everything imaginable. An abundance of social media sites exist to keep us connected and an overflow of applications to keep us organized. Who dares to say what technological innovation came into existence between the time I wrote this essay and its publication?

However, we must use these technologies with hopefulness and caution, with grace and thoughtfulness, with compassion and care.

Phones, computers, tablets, and other mobile devices have opened the world to us—their efficiency and helpfulness are quite enticing. At the same time, there is a danger in having too much information, too much meaningless interaction, too many shallow friendships online, and too many distractions from "real" life.

As people on the brink of careers in various forms of ministry, careers that intermingle the messiness of human life with the call of the Divine, we must be thoughtful in how we use and think about technology. While there are advantages to the marketing and selling that surround social media, excess in any form can be detrimental. Because there is so much the Internet can offer and because of its ubiquity, it is important for ministerial leaders in training to begin to practice thoughtful application and considered restraint. Clearly, these new technologies are a gift. For instance, there is an incredible number of websites, journals, and other resources readily available that in times past would have required innumerable trips to the library.

And yet we must remember that our use of social media is rooted in our social locations. We tend to socialize with people like us. It is this ontological sense of social identity that often drives theology, how we talk about God. Who we are correlates with our perception of who God is. Such theological underscoring informs whether individuals choose to use social media and particularly if they use it to market the message of God. This partnering of anthropology with theology also fashions the degree of technology's role in everyday life and in ministry.

In light of such a complex backdrop, this essay seeks to expound on the following matters: a theology of technology, the meaning of social in social media, and the maintenance of a sound mind in the midst of sound bytes. Individuals considering a career in ministry or who are clear about their calling or vocation already know that such paths lead to more socializing. Ministry calls us to form many relationships with many people on many different levels. Prior to the advent of social media, people gathered primarily at homes, restaurants, and churches. A lunch meeting or a dinner outing, an after-church meeting or after-school fellowship used to be the societal norm. Now, such socializing also occurs via computers and phones.

Yet to what extent are these interactions really social? And what happens when these interactions become convenient more than intentional? How can online evangelism, prayer over text message, or Bible study on Skype help minister to the needs of people and help you, the student, live out your call to serve God and humankind? And what are the limits of these new frontiers in social interaction?

Just as there is a need to consider what we mean by social, so also we need to examine how social media and God talk intersect in helpful ways sometimes or work at cross-purposes other times. After all, it is so easy to contact people via texts, e-mail, and webpages that such forms of social media and connectedness can both help ministers serve people in times of great need but also become all-consuming. The instant posts and responses can help us reach people near and far but also leave us wanting or needing more and more. If your ministerial calling is rooted in God, then we all must be careful that the hype of social media does not overwhelm God's small, still voice amidst so much Internet chatter and clutter. After all, if we are too distracted by the buzzing of our phones, we might just miss God speaking to us, whether by text or burning bush.

A Theology of Technology

Expounding on the connection of technology with our spiritual and social lives, Craig Detweiler maintains, "We cannot place our faith in technology as the solution to our congregational ills. We need a robust theology of technology to precede the adoption of lights, cameras, and action. Bigger, louder, and faster don't necessarily create deeper disciples."[1] He argues that the ubiquity of social media, apps, and all related tools not only inform how we think about God but also tailor our ability to relate to each other. How we view technology molds and shapes our view of God and God's creation. Our employment of Apple products and Microsoft deliverables speaks to what we do on the Sabbath as much as the things we do in church on Sunday mornings. This is the case at least according to Detweiler.

---

1. Craig Detweiler, *iGods: How Technology Shapes Our Spiritual and Social Lives* (Grand Rapids: Brazos, 2012), 28.

While there is much merit to Detweiler's argument, I asseverate that the beginning point of how we use technology is not technology itself but our convictions about God. Yes, the means by which we engage online offerings color how we live out who God is and whom God calls us to be. In fact, how we share the good news speaks volumes about our belief systems. A theology of technology purports that our understanding of God compels the disseminating of such by any means necessary. Because a person's comprehension of God leads him or her to share that knowledge in whatever forum or fashion, then technology becomes just as much an avenue for such expression as knocking on a door or attending a worship service. If God is everywhere, then the message about God's grace, love, and forgiveness must be shared everywhere, including the Internet.

Ministries tend to use the Internet for various reasons. For some churches, it is a matter of evangelism or sharing the gospel message. In addition, many pastors see the use of technology as a means of keeping in touch with parishioners throughout the week. For them, it is an opportunity to check in with members regularly. The use of social media becomes an extension of their shepherding. Furthermore, the sharing of information such as church events, schedule changes, and membership concerns can also be the impetus for such use.

While these are good reasons to use technology in ministry, it should be incumbent on churches and ministry leaders to discover and solidify their theology or belief system even as they dive into what can be the murky waters of the Internet. Reckless use of social media sites can lead to de-socialization. That is, excessive online presence can impair our ability to interact in person. Seminarians who are on the cusp of preparing for ministry should spend as much time discerning their theological struggles and stances as they do discerning how the Internet might be a safe, sound, and valuable place to engage in ministry. Equally true is that careful use of social networks can prove invaluable in helping people discern whom God is calling them to be and how God is calling them to be in (social) community.

A theology of technology encourages people of God to scrutinize first whom they perceive God to be in the world. It compels individuals to review their understanding of how God works today. Such a foundation does not begin with technology as a possible means for reaching God's people. It begins with God as the creator of all. It is rooted in trying to understand the message of God's love for humankind and then embodying that love through social connections.

While a theology of technology sets the stage for the inner work anyone in ministry should do, it also serves as a warning against the misuse of technology "in Jesus' name." Having taught undergraduate and graduate students, I unfortunately have had to deal with students in religious and theological studies who plagiarized assignments. I honestly do not think the students were bad or evil for doing so. After the first penalty, many did not cheat again or did not do so in my class at least. Yet quite often, lack of self-care, the availability of easily accessible materials on the Internet, and the ease of copying and pasting have made and still create a perfect plagiarizing storm. Plus, not everything online is true or accurate. Anyone can post a blog. A blog does not an expert make. Some of the material students plagiarize is not even worth repeating. Be forewarned.

Spending time working out, working through, working in one's theological core may preclude a church leader on the rise, a woman or man whom God has called, from abusing the Internet "for God's sake." After all, a theology of technology ought to reflect God and God's goodness. That's what techies do; they are artisans content with making others look good.[2]

The Social in Social Media

In her TED Talk, Sherry Turkle discusses how technology deceives us into believing that we are together. In fact, many of us are deeply connected to social media but alone in reality.[3] Social media sites have the ability to join people living in different time zones in one place at the same time. People in various parts of the world can come together to make business deals or just chat, due to the convenience afforded by Skype, FaceTime, Google Hangouts, and the like. Technology allows a woman in Birmingham to see and chat with a man in San Diego while also having a conversation via text with another person in Dayton. All of this meeting, liking, following, messaging, tweeting, and texting gives the impression that citizens are sociable and are in good social standing with one another. Because individuals spend so much time in contact with each other and can contact each other so readily, there is the tendency to think that everyone is at the center of many social circles.

We call this kind of interaction "social media." However, as people engaged in seminary and divinity school environments where reaching out to others is integral, we ought to strive for a fuller understanding of what it means to be social. "Social" means that we serve unique people with unique experiences who have unique ways of interpreting, living, doing, and being. To be in a social relationship with someone goes beyond retweeting or pinning items on a site. It is having a vested interest in the health, welfare, and spiritual development of the other. It is the ongoing, day-in and day-out, care and concern for people, their dreams and goals and where they are in life. Merely friending someone does not mean that one cares about that person's academic matriculation, family status,

---

2. Ibid., 24.

3. Sherry Turkle, "Connected, But Alone?," TED Talks, http://www.ted.com/talks/sherry_turkle_alone_together.

or cultural location. It does not mean that one is truly a friend or really wants to be friends with someone else. It is simply a click that allows for information exchange and a potential invasion of privacy. Certainly, such social webs can draw us into relationship with one another, but they are not a substitute for substantive relationships, online and offline.

But, no, the apps and social arrangements are not solely to blame. The fault lies with us. The ubiquity of our technologies only highlights our social tendencies. It does not create them. It can amplify our best and worst tendencies. And so we can only hope to connect with one another on social media if we remember the God whom we serve, a God who yearns that we love one another as sisters and brothers.

However, some of us have become computer literate and technologically savvy while suffering from arrested social development. Perchance the true indicator is this: If the persona I create online were to meet the real me, would the two know each other or would they pass by like two trains in the night? The life of the minister ought to be characterized by integrity. And so the life of the minister online must resonate with her everyday values and commitments.

As leaders for whom ministry and service to God is our way of life, the idea of being social must be rooted in what it means to be in community with the people of God. The task of anyone in ministry must be that of cultivating community. Of course, Jesus did not have access to the tools of technology present today, but the way he formed community can be an exemplar for our technological world. Jesus taught the physicality of social connections by touching lepers (Luke 5:13), manipulating withered hands (Luke 6:6), spitting on blinded eyes (John 9:6)—not that I recommend this necessarily—lifting the disabled (Luke 13:11), dining with various individuals (Mark 2:15), and having extended, face-to-face conversations in the heat of the day (John 4:7ff). The physicality of Jesus' ministry should lead us to wonder how digital technology might help us be an embodied, tangible presence in the life of those we serve, whether we are physically or digitally present.

A Sound Mind in the Midst of Sound Bytes

Entering the world of seminary and divinity school is a task unto itself. It involves learning a new language; reading the Bible from a more intense, academic perspective; and having to sit in periods of cognitive dissonance and questioning. These are just a few of the challenges of braving this new world. Trying to stay connected to friends, family, news events, and happenings across the globe can be overwhelming. The first section of this essay forwarded a theology that becomes the root for understanding how and why people use technology. As the previous section focused on understanding the presence and absence of social connections in social media, the next section turned to how we manage our social presence. Now, in this third section, we consider how periods of silence and sabbath from technology might also aid in theological development.

There is no elegant way to say this, so here it is: learn to turn it all off.

Become adept at turning the cell phone off when there is no pressing reason to be available. Develop a habit of occasionally but intentionally abstaining from e-mailing, texting, tweeting, blogging, pinning, or posting anything online. The constant use of technology can be addictive. The more one has of it, the more one will want of it. The reality is that social media can satisfy an individual only for a moment. It is as if you eat the breakfast of Facebook or the Chinese food of Instagram, and an hour or so later, you are hungry again. The empty social calories provided via so much Internet engagement can leave us wanting something more, even as we are surrounded by so many digital connections.

Learn to take a sabbath from it all.

The beauty and beast of the Internet is that the information never disappears, messages never stop arriving. There is always something else to read. Remaining spiritually sound while encircled and surrounded by so many Internet bits and pieces requires periods of silence. Sometimes, we just need moments to be.[4] All the noise of apps and the conversations from social media can send anyone into auditory and visual overload. A walk in the park, a run around the corner, or a short drive can heal the mind, body, and spirit. Listening to the birds or flowing water or just feeling the warmth of the sun has a way of reinvigorating the soul and reconnecting us to the God of heaven and earth. That is what the seminary journey is about for the most part. It is about taking the time to walk and commune with God in ways that you have not previously experienced. Refuse to let the cosmos of "www" hinder such time.

Moments away from social media can serve as opportunities to assess our use of it and perhaps its use of us. Time apart from social media often aids in evaluating its validity or importance in our life. A respite from the Internet and periods of silence can provide an arena for discovering what kind of social presence is integral to our callings. So often, people get online just to get online. Before we know it, the tail is wagging the dog or the app is running the individual.

---

4. Stephanie Buckhanon Crowder and Nyasha Junior, "Not Another New Year's Resolution," *Huffington Post*, http://www.huffingtonpost.com/nyasha-junior/not-another-new-years-res_b_4521035.html.

Conclusion

As an ordained clergywoman and professor, I see the value in technology and use it often in workshops and teaching moments. Yes, social media can be useful in dialoguing with like-minded academics and ministers. There is a degree of camaraderie in being "linked in" with an online group. Yet, this is not the extent of what it means to be social. The human touch and the human voice are still windows into the human heart. I believe this because my theology says this is who God is; this is what God did. God came in human form to reconcile humanity to God's self. It is invasion incarnation.[5] This is the message I want to give to the world, and the World Wide Web is one of a number of means I can use to translate this message.

Yet, I do so carefully and with prudence, lest while running the race I disqualify myself, lest while sharing the gospel online, I become overloaded. I strive not to have the massive offerings of the tools of technology overwhelm, over-app, or overtake me. Periods of rest and reflection restore my spirit and remind me of who and whose I am. People in the embryonic stages of their seminary careers would be wise to learn who they are in God's eyes and seek to connect with others online and offline but also unplug regularly, let technology go occasionally, and embrace times of simply be-ing.

This essay tries to offer insight on the pros and cons of online life in order to help seminarians navigate its technological terrain. The disadvantages are in many ways rooted in human nature. We must control what we post on the Internet, and we must control how long we click our way through its various offerings. Yet, the ease with which seminarians and anyone can engage in online research is grounded also in humans, people who have taken the time to make

5. Brian Blount, *Invasion of the Dead: Preaching Resurrection* (Louisville, KY: Westminster John Knox, 2014), 85.

various resources accessible. Technology allows pastors to market church events and support, if only from a distance, the work of their colleagues. Social media can be a forum for racially and socially diverse conversation partners to engage in extensive theological exchange. Social media can make virtually irrelevant whether people are in the same city, the same state, or even the same country. Actually, such geographical barriers make the use of social media in ministry and theological studies all the more exciting. Just think: one e-mail can allow a student to connect with an author or professor whether she is enrolled in the teacher's class or not. This indeed speaks to the power of thinking and living socially.

Many disagree about what the church's engagement with social media ought to be. For some, these digital networks are holy ground. For others, these digital networks unveil the darkest corners of humanity. They may both be right. Perhaps, though, the Internet and the social connections it enables are neither perfect nor irretrievably corrupt. Perhaps they are as flawed and as wonderful, as human and as divine as any interaction between people who are sinners and saints alike.

9

Thinking Spiritually

Cláudio Carvalhaes

How do we measure our spirituality? When is it that we can start *thinking spiritually*? Is it the Spirit that affects our thinking, or is it our thinking that defines our spirituality?

At the heart of our spiritualities (note the plural use of the word; we will come back to this), we will find our bodies. It is in our bodies, in their possibilities *and* limitations, that we think spiritually, experience meaning, and sense God in the wide array of our spiritualities. Our bodies carry the memories of our existence. Our memories record the cartography of the many movements of the Holy Spirit in our lives. It is exactly *in* our bodies that we are spirit. Our flesh and bones are living documents that constantly receive, apprehend, learn, and challenge this faith we once received.

This is why I decided to use the *bodyography* of my life during my seminary years to reflect on what it means to think spiritually. The history of my body is the history of my faith and the history of my spiritualities. Where my body has been, with whom it related (individually and in community), where it sweat and cried, where it hurt and shouted for joy, these places and situations and circumstances carry the multiple identities of my body and the history of God in my life.

When I write about bodyography, I must begin in an immemorial time, when God called me God's own. This calling was celebrated in my baptism, and in this ritual of remembrance, the history of my life was already rewritten, backward and forward, reshaping my past and opening up the future. Thus, past and future meet my present in the very breathing of my body. My body (and yours) has always been the locus of God's epiphanies. My bodyography is thus the movement of the Spirit in my body. This rejects any separation of my body and my spirit, setting me free to experience God in the flesh of my body, always in relation to others and to the earth.

If you are to think about your spirituality through the history of your body, what are the places, memories, tattoos, joys, embarrassments, illnesses, sexual encounters, ideas of God, interpretations of the Bible, moral codes, and social situations that you can recount? What does your faith have to do with all of these moments? At the end of this essay, I will ask you to write your own bodyography, to try to perceive where your body has been in your life and the several markers that make you who you are at this juncture in your life.

As a Latin American, I have learned that I think with my feelings and feel with my thinking. By trying to recount my spiritual life through my bodyography, I hope you will see that thinking, living, feeling, that is, experiencing the Spirit in our lives, comprise one whole, interconnected event.

When I think theologically about the Spirit, I think about God's many names and the many ways God draws our bodies, our lives, and our communities together. The Christian faith is a religion of the flesh, *in-carne*, incarnated. Emmanuel, "God with us!" Christianity is about a God who becomes flesh and bone, and in the flesh, God discovers, lives, enacts, wrestles, receives, and gives the Spirit. Every bit of theological thinking must be done in, from, and through many bodies: our own, the bodies of the poor, and the body of Christ himself.

Thinking Spiritually When I Didn't Know I Was Thinking Spiritually

During my teenage years I was restless about my faith. I always wanted to learn about and experience more of my faith, and so I spent lots of time with American parachurch groups, like Youth with a Mission and Bill Bright's Campus Crusade for Christ. My evangelistic zeal made me want to tell the whole world the good news of Jesus Christ. I wanted to be like Billy Graham. My body needed energy, movement, something that would give me a mission in life.

However, even though I was exploring other churches and getting to know other groups, I never left my home church. That church was my nest, the community where my body had a place to be and to grow freely. In that community I found a net of support to try things out, because I knew my church would be there for me. I was never afraid of trying different things, of taking risks, because I knew they loved me and would never let me go.

My church nurtured my spirituality even when we disagreed. When I was seventeen, my church silenced me for a whole year after I preached a sermon about social action. To say the least, the sermon didn't go over well. For a year I couldn't teach, lead worship, or preach. But I could pray! Much later I learned that the famous Brazilian theologian Leonardo Boff was silenced by his beloved Roman Catholic Church. In response, he said these famous words: "I prefer to walk with the church rather than to walk alone with my theology."[1]

When my church sanctioned me, I didn't even think about leaving. Where would I go? How would I live without them? I wasn't ready to fly away from my nest. They had formed me so deeply, and without them I couldn't breathe the Spirit anymore. My own thinking, living, breathing, and sweating of the Spirit was so deeply connected with my people that we were a *familia*, a family. We were bound less by a denominational identity or a proper confession of faith than by our living together, our sheltering and nurturing one another by the power of the Spirit.

However, in the midst of this crisis, I had to ask hard questions. Was the Spirit with me, or was I going beyond acceptable theological thinking? Was my thinking drifting away from the spirit of God? If preaching is the word of God, what happened that morning? Was the word of God not preached that morning? Why did my leaders silence me? The conundrums, crossroads, and paradoxes of spirituality were finally becoming clear to me.

Later that year I decided to go to seminary. In Brazil you can attend seminary right after high school. But then when I was about to go, I had yet another problem: even though I had been working since I was thirteen years old, I didn't have enough money to pay for my education. When I mentioned this financial shortfall to my church and my presbytery, they agreed to pay my tuition. And so the same church that one year before had silenced me decided, now, to support me.

These were historical marks in the cartography of God's spirit acting in my life, tattoos of God's love marking all the layers of my

---

1. Leonardo Boff, "*Esclarecimento de Leonardo Boff às preocupações da Congregação para a Doutrina da Fé acerca do livro Igreja: Carisma e poder* (1981)," in *Igreja: Carisma e poder. Ensaios de eclesiologia militante de Frei Leonardo Boff* (Petrópolis: Vozes, 1985), 334.

skin and my spirit, my *comunidade*—my community—embodying the work of the Spirit in my life.

My Body against the Spirit

At that time in my life what it meant to think spiritually was not well defined in my *head*. Instead, I now see that everything I was experiencing was all tied together in my body, a certain "unbearable lightness of [my] being"[2] in the midst of God's possible call, my community's presence, and my own journey.

But when I got to seminary I was carrying a deeply dualistic view of body and spirit. Throughout my upbringing, body and spirit were at odds with each other. Spirituality was associated with proper thinking, which meant proper behavior, which itself required the consequent demise of my body. I knew I had to cast away the weight of my flesh and all its desires, including the sexual desires that pulsed vividly in every pore of my body. I was taught that to be closer to God I had to deny my body. To live in my flesh—my body—was to live away from God's spirit. In my early theological formation, spirit and flesh did not communicate, and one lived by the necessary destruction of the other. This dualistic view linked my spirit with God and my body with the devil. In the midst of this dualistic theology, I had to deal with my failures, deep frustrations, and growing incapacity to please God with my life.

This war between flesh and spirit is not only destructive to people's subjectivities and interpersonal relations but can also subvert faithful ways of living. After all, our refusal to live with those we disagree with, those we don't like, or those we refuse to understand mirrors this battle between good and bad, spirit and flesh.

2. Milan Kundera, *The Unbearable Lightness of Being: A Lover's Story* (New York: Perennial Classics, 1999).

My spirituality was a way of working against my flesh and my evangelistic zeal an outward sign that proved my faith was beating up my body. It was and has been a long journey to undo this dichotomy and engage flesh and spirit, thinking and emotions as one blessed, interrelated event.

My Body Caught Up in Other Theological Dichotomies

Unfortunately, this dichotomy between body and spirit can also appear in seminary education. One form this dichotomy takes has to do with the relationship between clergy and laity. Some schools of thought can teach us that we shouldn't place much trust in the laity and that the very purpose of ministry was *clergy* teaching, *clergy* organizing the church, *clergy* leading worship, and *clergy* helping people to go about their lives. In some ways, the biblical illiteracy of many church people has to do with a deep distrust that clergy hold of the laity. At core, we don't believe that our people can actually do things. We clergy tend to see our people as biblically, spiritually, theologically, and liturgically needy. We tend to think that what they need is *our* ministry when really the *Spirit* already empowers us all.

For example, there is a widespread notion in the church and academy alike that liturgy is to be done *on behalf* of the people *by* the ministerial leaders and not *by and for* the people. If the former is true, then people are supposed to watch clergy do the liturgy for them and merely follow what the clergy tells them to do. That mistrust comes also from the belief that we can't trust people to hold what is sacred. That many people in so many Christian denominations don't know how to pray extemporaneously, that people are not even allowed to hold the bread of the Eucharist, or that people's stories aren't taken seriously shows that we believe the Spirit abides with the clergy. In this way, we train our bodies to remain on the margins of worship and away from the holiest places. In this way, we end up not trusting fully in the work of the Spirit in our bodies, spirits, and minds.

These assumptions reflect the hierarchical business model that has taken over our churches and turned pastors into CEOs and people into customers. In this model, pastors are supposed to do everything *for* the people: worship, administer the church, counsel, and teach the Bible. In this way, people are trained to be recipients of a certain knowledge. This liturgical, biblical, theological, business, and educational approach is what the Brazilian educational theorist Paulo Freire calls a "banking model": "Education thus becomes an act of depositing, in which students are the depositories and the teacher is the depositor. . . . In the banking concept of education, knowledge is a gift bestowed by those who consider themselves knowledgeable upon those whom they consider to know nothing."[3] This sense of education maintains a disconnect between body and spirit, community and individual, and creates a hierarchical structure that undermines a community of people who can teach and learn together. That disconnect can also be seen in seminaries. Seminary education will surely appeal to your mind and to your thinking, though sometimes that same education will neglect your body and how your body is fundamental to creating and engaging your spirituality.

My Seminary Years

Coming from a church heavily influenced by a mixture of conservatism and fundamentalism, I remember feeling scared in some of my seminary classes.[4] I had several challenges studying at a more

---

3. Paulo Freire, *Pedagogy of the Oppressed*, trans. Myra B. Ramos (1968; repr., London: Penguin Books, 1996), 53.

liberal seminary, especially in my first two years. In some instances, it felt like I was expanding, but mostly I felt like the ground was disappearing under my feet. The anxiety of going to classes, the fear of not being able to do the work, the feeling that I was not good enough or smart enough, and the uncertainty of God's call made my body live in a convoluted state for some time.

After a short time, I started feeling estranged from my church. What I was reading and discussing was not even close to what my church was reading and discussing, and I felt I had moved somewhere else. It was as if my church and I were now living in two different worlds. This estrangement continued for many years. Eventually, however, I realized that if what I was learning did not empower my own people, there was no point to what I was studying.

At some point during seminary, I went through a personal crisis. I started to ask myself if I actually had a call to ministry or if it was a product of my church upbringing. I had embraced a kind of savior complex, but I didn't realize it until I was in seminary, and so my understanding of my call started to unravel. The important decisions I needed to make were fast approaching, and I dreaded facing them with only my own strength and natural ability. I didn't know what to think or feel, and my body felt the consequences of this battle of discernment. Neither prayers nor readings fixed what was broken or moved the process along. Looking back, I can now see that I needed to linger a little longer in a place of uncertainty and that meaning, absurdity, and paradoxes were the very content of this faith. My spirit and body were battling with these tensions, and through time, I felt a change, though one that I couldn't name just yet.

---

4. Seminary took me about five years because all my coursework was done in the evening. Working during the day from 8:00 a.m. to 6:00 p.m., I would then attend seminary classes from 7:00 to 10:30 p.m. These were hard and joyful times, times when most of my homework was done on the bus coming and going to the seminary.

I was able to go through this process only because I had people caring deeply for my whole well-being. As I started the last year of my seminary studies, I was shocked when the registrar told me that my presbytery had decided to withdraw support from all ministerial candidates due to financial constraints it was experiencing. The news felt like a sign that I should have never gone to seminary in the first place. That was it. I decided to quit my studies.

But Lauro Ferreira, now in his eighties, came to me after a worship service in our church and said to me, "I heard you are quitting seminary. Don't do that. Go back to school tomorrow!" And I said, "Mr. Lauro, I cannot afford it." He said, "Go back to school tomorrow." And I repeated, "But Mr. Lauro . . ." He interrupted me again and said, "Son, didn't I tell you to go back to school tomorrow?" And I said, "Okay." The next day, I went to the seminary not knowing what I was doing. I approached our beloved registrar, saying, "Ms. Neusa, I came just to bid you farewell. I am quitting seminary since I can't afford it." She replied, "Why? An elder of your church came here this morning and paid for the entire year of your studies."

My community, the body of Christ, was once again responding, sustaining my body, supporting the movements of my faith, showing that in many ways the conditions of my spirituality were possible only when I lived in connection, in *familia*, in *comunidad*. My body felt a flush of joy and gratitude that I can still feel today. This was the Spirit! The Spirit was moving in me through the cloud of witnesses, the church of Jesus Christ. The flux of the Spirit in my body connected me to a larger sense of what it is to be a follower of Jesus. Up to this day, when I go to our little Presbyterian church, I approach Mr. Lauro after I preach and say, "Mr. Lauro, you changed my life." And he always replies, "You have to improve your sermons!"

Our Bodies Are Where We Begin Thinking Spiritually

Every spirituality is political. How so?

If our spiritualities happen in our bodies, we must consider how our bodies are the cartography of God's manifestations. The cartography of our bodies is marked by the maps we learn along the way. The maps, our bodies, are the places where the social and the political happen, and that means our behavior, sexualities, social life, moral codes, and ethical commitments happen in a community marked by certain maps. Whose voices are speaking in your community and forming these maps? Is there a diversity of voices in the composition of these maps? How are our theologies performed or embodied in your church or seminary? What voices are telling you about how you can think about, relate to, or experience God? For instance, if you go to a seminary where there is no diversity of voices, you might think that your body and your spirituality must comply only with the maps shown to you. You might never know and feel that there are many spiritualities and many forms of diversity where God lives.

The Salvadorian theologian Jon Sobrino talks about spirituality in relation to "political holiness."[5] With this term, he wants to convey the sense that our faith is marked by the presence of the Spirit. The spirit of the church of Jesus Christ, engaged in the struggles for the sake of the poor, can politically and socially transform the world. "Political holiness" as it relates to the Christian faith entails a sense of historical efficacy in what it does and represents to the world. The Spirit that lives in our bodies cannot be vague or indifferent to the political–economic system of our present age.

---

5. Jon Sobrino, *Spirituality of Liberation: Toward Political Holiness* (Maryknoll, NY: Orbis Books, 1988), 83.

To live a spiritual, "political holiness" means to gain a spiritual sense of the practices of the polis, of the city, but also of the social, cultural, and economic structures and practices of the church. Sobrino notes, "Without spirit, practice degenerates. Without practice, spirit remains vague, indifferent, even alienated."[6] That means our bodies and spiritual practices are not disassociated from the social-political life of our societies, churches, and seminaries. Our spiritual practices are exercises of a faith marked by the social conditions and theological possibilities we encounter.

The Anglican Brazilian theologian Jaci Maraschin once argued that "the theme of the body has always been present in the theology of creation, in the treatise of incarnation (Christology), in the debates around human realities, in the consideration of sin and fall, in the themes related to the sacramental life of the church, and finally in the doctrine of the resurrection of Jesus Christ and our own resurrection."[7] Maraschin goes beyond that to say, "It is in the body that we are Spirit."[8]

By saying this, he is trying to break the dichotomy of body and spirit many of us have inherited, a dichotomy that elevates spirit over body, making the body a negative place. We need to rescue the sense, importance, and fundamental connection of the body to the spirit in order to think spiritually. It is in the flesh that I can touch, feel, smell, hear, taste, and see the Spirit. Away from my body or the bodies of my brothers and sisters around the world, and especially the bodies of the poor, I have no idea where the Spirit might be.[9]

---

6. Ibid., ix.
7. Jaci C. Maraschin, "Fé Cristã e Corpo," in *Fé cristã: libertação do cativeiro para a esperança.* Cadernos de Pós-Graduação, Ciências da Religião (5). (SBCampo: Programa Ecumênico de Pós-Graduação em Ciências da Religião, junho de 1986), 57.
8. Jaci C. Maraschin, "*É no corpo que somos Espírito,*" unpublished, 12.
9. Marcella Althaus-Reid goes even further that to say that every theology is sexual, markedly done by certain sexual performances of the theologians. There is no way to think spiritually about God, faith, and our whole lives without first attending, attesting, and paying attention

The body as a locus of God's manifestation becomes the starting point of our theologies. After all, it is in the body that God in Jesus re-creates life for all of us! As Maraschin says, "It is in the body that we are spirit, especially when the body re-creates life. Let us make the body our fundamental instrument of adoration."[10]

Conclusion

Now that I am a professor in a seminary, I strive to help my students discern more clearly their call, their thinking, their spirituality, and their bodies. When I asked Elyssa E. Salinas, one of my students at Lutheran Theological Seminary at Philadelphia, to write about this complicated relationship, she decided to use baptism as her starting point and wrote a beautiful poem:

Bath

So I come back to my room.
I sink into the tub and
Wrap myself in a watery memory.
A time when I was told that I was loved
With no tests or trials.
Just a watery kiss on my forehead.

Only water I feel safe in
I want to be drenched & come up dripping.

When the water leaves I feel heavy &
I like it.

to our bodies and our sexualities. See Marcella Althaus-Reid, *Indecent Theology: Theological Perversions in Sex, Gender, and Politics* (London: Routledge, 2000).
10. Maraschin, "*É no corpo que somos Espírito*," 12.

Finally I feel my weight.
The heaviness of being human,
Too big & bold to be sucked down a drain.
I like the feeling of weight, of pressure on me.
The weight makes me stay put,
Place my pen on paper, my eyes on words &
my ears in the presence of others.
Makes me stay in the class,
At the stained glass,
And in the calling I hear so strongly.
The weight that makes my feet sink into the floor
as I step out & step away
From all that has been washed off me.
All the doubt and questioning.
It has all been sucked down the drain &
All that is left of me is the weight of me;
With hair in knots & shades of black traveling down my face.
No perfect picture of my flawless face &
Modest towel to cover me up.

Here I am.
Dripping in my skin & rejoicing in the weight of me.[11]

Perhaps Elyssa's poem can help us start to figure out what thinking spiritually might be all about. She is connecting her body with her body in a bath. These waters might have been the memory of her baptism, and she feels safe there. From there, she senses her body. In her body, she is learning and engaging her faith. In the weight of her body, she discovers the limits and the possibilities of her spirituality.

11. Elyssa Salinas, "*Bath,*" April 16, 2014.

I invite you to do the same. Write your own *bodyography* and try to perceive where your body has been in your life. When you do this, search for the following marks that might be present in your body:

- Biblical marks: What are some of the body images you see in the Bible?
- Personal marks: Do you accept, love, and celebrate your body?
- Theological marks: How do you see God viewing and relating to your body?
- Cultural marks: Is your body something to be mistrusted or embraced?
- Ethical marks: How do our societies morally define your body and your sexualities?
- Social marks: Does your body have access to everything? What bodies are either erased or placed under the shadow of anonymity in our societies?
- Political marks: How does your local and federal government honor or dismiss, exploit or protect the body of its people?
- Economic marks: What are the companies that own our bodies? Think about the marketing industry: cosmetics, clothes, agribusiness, food production, social media, and so on.

After you do that, be aware of your theological education. Don't let yourself be trapped in the facile and unavailing dichotomies of spirit and body, personal and social, thinking and feeling, evangelism and social action. These are not mutually exclusive options but potentially integrated wholes. Your theology must embrace nothing less than your entire life.

My hope is that you will be able to perceive the movements of the Spirit in every movement of your body as it is connected with your own context and history, and how you love and are loved, how you struggle, fear, and keep going. May your thinking spiritually expand far beyond looking for spirituality only in times of contemplation or retreat or aha moments. Thinking spiritually is much more ordinary than that, and for that reason, much more powerful.

More Thinking

This book is only the beginning. When you are read to reflect more on what it means to think theologically, we commend the following texts to you.

Althaus-Reid, Marcella. *Indecent Theology, Theological Perversions in Sex, Gender, and Politics.* New York: Routledge, 2000.

Alves, Rubem. *I Believe in the Resurrection of the Body.* Eugene, OR: Wipf and Stock, 2003.

Anderson, Keith and Elizabeth Dresher. *Click 2 Save: The Digital Ministry Bible.* Harrisburg, PA: Morehouse, 2012.

Barth, Karl. *The Humanity of God.* Louisville, KY: Westminster John Knox, 1960.

Blount, Brian. *Invasion of the Dead: Preaching Resurrection.* Louisville, KY: Westminster John Knox, 2014.

Brueggemann, Walter. *The Prophetic Imagination.* 2nd ed. Minneapolis: Augsburg Fortress, 2001.

Cone, James. *God of the Oppressed.* Maryknoll, NY: Orbis, 1997.

Crowder, Stephanie Buckhanon and Nyasha Junior. "Not Another New Year's Resolution." *Huffington Post.* http://www.huffingtonpost.com/nyasha-junior/not-another-new-years-res_b_4521035.html.

Detweiler, Craig. *iGods: How Technology Shapes Our Spiritual and Social Lives.* Grand Rapids: Brazos, 2012.

Gould, Meredith. *The Word Made Fresh: Communicating Church and Faith Today.* Harrisburg, PA: Morehouse, 2008.

Gutiérrez, Gustavo. *A Theology of Liberation: History, Politics, and Salvation.* Maryknoll, NY: Orbis, 1988.

Humphrey, Edith M. *Grand Entrance: Worship on Earth as in Heaven.* Grand Rapids: Brazos, 2011.

Johnson, Elizabeth. *She Who Is: The Mystery of God in Feminist Theological Discourse.* New York: Crossroad, 2002.

Malphurs, Aubrey. *Look Before You Lead: How to Discern and Shape Your Church Culture.* Grand Rapids: Baker, 2013.

Osmer, Richard R. *Practical Theology: An Introduction.* Grand Rapids: Eerdmans, 2008.

Patterson, Kerry and Joseph Grenny, et al. *Crucial Conversations: Tools for Talking When the Stakes Are High.* New York: McGraw Hill, 2012.

Pohl, Christian D. *Living into Community: Cultivating Practices That Sustain Us.* Grand Rapids: Eerdmans, 2012.

Provan, Iain. *Seriously Dangerous Religion: What the Old Testament Says and Why It Matters.* Waco, TX: Baylor University Press, 2014.

Smith, James K. A. *Desiring the Kingdom: Worship, Worldview, and Cultural Formation.* Grand Rapids: Baker Academic, 2009.

———. *Imagining the Kingdom: How Worship Works.* Grand Rapids: Baker Academic, 2013.

Turkle, Sherry. "Connected, But Alone?" TED Talks. http://www.ted.com/talks/sherry_turkle_alone_together.

Williams, Rowan. *Why Study the Past? The Quest for the Historical Church.* Grand Rapids: Eerdmans, 2005.

Wilken, Robert Louis. *Remembering the Christian Past.* Grand Rapids: Eerdmans, 1995.

Wright, N. T. *After You Believe: Why Christian Character Matters.* New York: Harper Collins, 2010.

Bibliography

Althaus-Reid, Marcella. *Indecent Theology: Theological Perversions in Sex, Gender, and Politics*. London: Routledge, 2000.

Augustine. *De doctrina Christiana*, translated and edited by R. P. H. Green. Oxford: Clarendon Press, 1995.

Ayres, Lewis. *Nicaea and Its Legacy: An Approach to Fourth-Century Trinitarian Theology*. Oxford: Oxford University Press, 2004.

Barna, George. *Futurecast: What Today's Trends Mean for Tomorrow's World*. Austin, TX: Tyndale, 2011.

Barth, Karl. "The Word of God as the Task of Theology." In *The Word of God and Theology*, translated by Amy Marga, 171-198. T&T Clark Studies in Systematic Theology. New York: Bloomsbury, 2011.

Bauckham, Richard. *James: The Wisdom of James, Disciple of Jesus the Sage*. London: Routledge, 1999.

Boff, Leonardo. "*Esclarecimento de Leonardo Boff às preocupações da Congregação para a Doutrina da Fé acerca do livro Igreja: Carisma e poder (1981).*" In *Igreja: Carisma e poder. Ensaios de eclesiologia militante de Frei Leonardo Boff*, 277-334. Petrópolis: Vozes, 1985.

Bonhoeffer, Dietrich. *Letters and Papers from Prison*. New York: Simon and Schuster, 1997.

————. *The Cost of Discipleship*. Norwich: SCM Press, 2001.

Bradshaw, Paul F. *Reconstructing Early Christian Worship*. Collegeville, MN: Liturgical Press, 2009.

Breuggemann, Walter. "Biblical Authority." *The Christian Century* (January 3–10, 2001): 14–20.

Blount, Brian. *Invasion of the Dead: Preaching Resurrection.* Louisville, KY: Westminster John Knox,

Brock, Rita and Rebecca Parker. *Proverbs of Ashes: Violence, Redemptive Suffering and the Search for What Saves Us.* Boston: Beacon Press, 2001.

Buckhanon Crowder, Stephanie and Nyasha Junior. "Not Another New Year's Resolution." *Huffington Post.* Accessed August 25, 2014. http://www.huffingtonpost.com/nyasha-junior/not-another-new-years-res_b_4521035.html.

Cahalan, Kathleen A. and James R. Nieman. "Mapping the Field of Practical Theology," in *For Life Abundant: Practical Theology, Theological Education, and Christian Ministry*, ed. Dorothy C. Bass and Craig Dykstra, 62-90. Grand Rapids: Eerdmans, 2008.

Charry, Ellen. *By the Renewing of Your Minds: The Pastoral Function of Christian Doctrine.* New York: Oxford University Press, 1997.

Clines, David J. A. "Biblical Hermeneutics in Theory and Practice." *Christian Brethren Review* 31, 32 (1982): 65–76.

Coakley, Sarah. *God, Sexuality, and the Self: An Essay 'On the Trinity'.* Cambridge: Cambridge University Press, 2013.

Cone, James. *The Cross and the Lynching Tree.* Maryknoll, NY: Orbis Books, 2011.

Daly, Lois K. *Feminist Theological Ethics: A Reader.* Louisville, KY: Westminster John Knox, 1994.

De La Torre, Miguel. *Doing Christian Ethics from the Margins.* Maryknoll, NY: Orbis, 2004.

————. *Handbook on U.S. Theologies of Liberation.* St. Louis: Chalice Press, 2004.

Detweiler, Craig. *iGods: How Technology Shapes Our Spiritual and Social Lives.* Grand Rapids: Brazos, 2012.

Duckworth, Jessicah Krey. *Wide Welcome: How the Unsettling Presence of Newcomers Can Save the Church.* Minneapolis: Fortress Press, 2013.

Dykstra, Craig. "Pastoral and Ecclesial Imagination." In *For Life Abundant: Practical Theology, Theological Education, and Christian Ministry*, edited by Dorothy C. Bass and Craig Dykstra, 41–61. Grand Rapids: Eerdmans, 2008.

The Episcopal Church. *Book of Common Prayer*. New York: Seabury Press, 1976.

"Fountain Lady Fights Back." *Good Morning America*. Accessed August 25, 2014. http://lybio.net/cathy-cruz-marrero-good-morning-america-fountain-lady-fights-back-lawsuit/people/.html.

Freire, Paulo. *Pedagogy of the Oppressed*. Translated by Myra B. Ramos. London: Penguin Books, 1996.

Grant, Jacquelyn. *White Women's Christ and Black Women's Jesus: Feminist Christology and Womanist Response*. Atlanta: Scholars Press, 1989.

Gutiérrez, Gustavo. *A Theology of Liberation: History, Politics and Salvation*. Maryknoll, NY: Orbis Books, 1973.

Lee, Hak Joon. *We Will Get to the Promised Land: Martin Luther King, Jr.'s Communal-Political Spirituality*. Cleveland: Pilgrim, 2006.

Instone-Brewer, David. *Divorce and Remarriage in the Bible*. Grand Rapids: Eerdmans, 2002.

Isasi-Díaz, Ada María. *Mujerista Theology: A Theology for the Twenty-first Century*. Maryknoll, NY: Orbis Books, 1996.

Janz, Denis, ed. *A People's History of Christianity*, 7 vols. Minneapolis: Fortress, 2005–2010.

Johnson, Elizabeth. *She Who Is: The Mystery of God in Feminist Theological Discourse*. New York: Crossroad, 1992.

Jones, Serene. *Trauma and Grace: Theology in a Ruptured World*. Louisville, KY: Westminster John Knox Press, 2009.

Jordan, Patrick, ed. *Dorothy Day: Writings from Commonweal*. Collegeville, MN: Liturgical Press, 2002.

Justin Martyr. *The First and Second Apologies*. Translated by Leslie W. Barnard. New York: Paulist Press, 1997.

Kearney, Richard. *Anatheism: Returning to God after God*. New York: Columbia University Press, 2010.

Kolb, Robert, James Schaffer, and Timothy Wengert, eds. *The Book of Concord*, 2nd ed. Minneapolis: Fortress Press, 2000.

Kundera, Milan. *The Unbearable Lightness of Being: A Lover's Story*. New York: Perennial Classics, 1999.

Lathrop, Gordon. *Central Things: Worship in Word and Sacrament*. Minneapolis: Augsburg Fortress, 2010.

López Vigil, Jose María. *Oscar Romero: Memories in Mosaic*. Translated by Kathy Ogle. Washington, DC: EPICA, 2000.

Loughlin, Gerard, ed. *Queer Theology: Rethinking the Western Body*. Malden, MA: Blackwell, 2007.

Maraschin, Jaci C. "Fé Cristã e Corpo." In *Fé cristã: libertação do cativeiro para a esperança*. Cadernos de Pós-Graduação, Ciências da Religião (5). (SBCampo: Programa Ecumênico de Pós-Graduação em Ciências da Religião, junho de 1986), 57.

————. "*É no corpo que somos Espírito*," unpublished, 12.

Marty, Peter W. "Shaping Communities: Pastoral Leadership and Congregational Formation." In *For Life Abundant: Practical Theology, Theological Education, and Christian Ministry*, ed. Dorothy C. Bass and Craig Dykstra, 306-328. Grand Rapids: Eerdmans, 2008.

Miller-McLemore, Bonnie J. *Christian Theology in Practice: Discovering a Discipline*. Grand Rapids: Eerdmans, 2012.

Moltmann, Jürgen, and Jürgen Weissbach. *Two Studies in the Theology of Bonhoeffer*. Translated by Reginald H. Fuller and Ilse Fuller. New York: Scribner, 1967.

Moon, Richard, ed. *Law and Religious Pluralism in Canada*. Vancouver, BC: UBC Press, 2008. Accessed August 25, 2014. http://www.ubcpress.ca/books/pdf/chapters/2008/LawandReligiousPluralisminCanada.pdf.html.

Mootz, Francis J. III, and George H. Taylor, eds. *Gadamer and Ricouer: Critical Horizons for Contemporary Hermeneutics*. New York: Continuum, 2011.

Musgrove, Laurence. "What Happens When We Read: Picturing a Reader's Responsibilities." *JAEPL* 11 (Winter 2005–2006): 52–63.

Osmer, Richard R. *Practical Theology: An Introduction.* Grand Rapids: Eerdmans, 2008.

Padgett, A. G. "Marcion." In *Dictionary of the Later New Testament and Its Developments.* Edited by Ralph P. Martin and Peter H. Davids. Downers Grove, IL: InterVarsity, 1997.

Provan, Iain. *Convenient Myths: The Axial Age, Dark Green Religion, and the World That Never Was.* Waco, TX: Baylor University Press, 2013.

Rajkumar, Peniel. *Dalit Theology and Dalit Liberation: Problems, Paradigms, and Possibilities.* Surrey: Ashgate, 2010.

Root, Andrew. *Christopraxis: A Practical Theology of the Cross.* Minneapolis: Fortress Press, 2014.

Rorem, Paul. "Empathy and Evaluation in Medieval Church History and Pastoral Ministry: A Lutheran Reading of Pseudo-Dionysius," *Princeton Seminary Bulletin* 19, no. 2 (1998): 99–115.

Rowe, Kavin. *World Upside Down: Reading Acts in the Graeco-Roman Age.* Oxford: Oxford University Press, 2010.

Rutba House, eds. *School(s) for Conversion: 12 Marks of a New Monasticism.* Eugene, OR: Wipf and Stock, 2005.

Saliers, Don E. *Worship as Theology: Foretaste of Glory Divine.* Nashville: Abingdon, 1994.

Salinas, Elyssa. "*Bath*," April 16, 2014.

Schmemann, Alexander. *For the Life of the World: Sacraments and Orthodoxy.* Crestwood, NY: St. Vladimir's Seminary Press, 2002.

Shannon, William H. *Witness to Freedom: The Letters of Thomas Merton in Times of Crisis.* New York: Farrar, Straus & Giroux, 1994.

Smart, Ninian. *The Religious Experience of Mankind.* Englewood Cliffs, NJ: Prentice Hall, 1969.

Smith, Christian. *Souls in Transition: The Religious and Spiritual Lives of Emerging Adults.* Oxford: Oxford University Press, 2009.

Smith, James K. A. *Desiring the Kingdom: Worship, Worldview, and Cultural Formation.* Grand Rapids: Baker Academic, 2009.

———. *Imagining the Kingdom: How Worship Works.* Grand Rapids: Baker Academic, 2013.

Sobrino, Jon. *Spirituality of Liberation: Toward Political Holiness*. Maryknoll, NY: Orbis Books, 1988.

Stahl, Bob and Elisha Goldstein. *A Mindfulness-Based Stress Reduction Workbook*. Oakland: New Harbinger, 2010.

Stone, Howard W. and James O. Duke. *How to Think Theologically*. Minneapolis: Fortress Press, 1996.

Thomas Aquinas. *Summa Contra Gentiles*, Bk. 1, Ch. 13. http://dhspriory.org/thomas/ContraGentiles.htm.

———. *Summa Theologica*, http://www.ccel.org/ccel/aquinas/summa.toc.html.

Tillich, Paul. *Systematic Theology*, Volume 1. Chicago: University Of Chicago Press, 1973.

Turkle, Sherry. "Connected, But Alone?," TED Talks. Accessed August 25, 2014. http://www.ted.com/talks/sherry_turkle_alone_together.

von Balthasar, Hans Urs. *The Glory of the Lord: A Theological Aesthetics*, ed. Joseph Fessio and John Kenneth Riches, vol. 1, *Seeing the Form*. San Francisco: Ignatius, 1982, 18-19.

Walls, Andrew. *The Missionary Movement in Christian History*. Maryknoll, NY: Orbis, 1996.

West, Traci. *Disruptive Christian Ethics: When Racism and Women's Lives Matter*. Louisville, KY: Westminster John Knox, 2006.

Williams, Dolores S. *Sisters in the Wilderness: The Challenge of Womanist God-Talk*. Maryknoll, NY: Orbis, 1993.

Wilson-Hartgrove, Jonathan. *New Monasticism: What It Has to Say to Today's Church*. Grand Rapids: Brazos, 2008.

Wogaman, J. Phillip. *Christian Ethics: A Historical Introduction*. Louisville, KY: Westminster John Knox, 1993.

Wright, N. T. *Paul and the Faithfulness of God, Book I*. Minneapolis: Fortress Press, 2013.

Yong, Amos. *The Spirit Poured Out on All Flesh: Pentecostalism and the Possibility of Global Theology*. Grand Rapids: Baker Academic, 2005.

———. *Spirit of Love: A Trinitarian Theology of Grace*. Waco, TX: Baylor University Press, 2012.